DEBRETT'S

MANNERS FOR MEN
what women really want

Debrett's Manners for Men
Published by Debrett's Limited
18–20 Hill Rise, Richmond,
Surrey TW10 6UA
United Kingdom

Managing Editor Jo Bryant

Editorial Assistants Sarah Corney, Ellie Major

Development Eleanor Mathieson

Proof reading and index Ruth Massey

Head of Publishing Elizabeth Wyse

Concept and style Warm Rain
Page design Design 23
Cover design LASH&KO

Creative Concept Ian Castello-Cortes
at Korero Books LLP, London

Published in association with ACC Publishing Group

Sandy Lane, Old Martlesham, Woodbridge,
Suffolk, IP12 4SD United Kingdom
www.antiquecollectorsclub.com

ISBN 978-1-85149-574-0

Printed and bound in China

Visit us at www.debretts.co.uk

MANNERS FOR MEN
what women really want

E. JANE DICKSON

DEBRETT'S

Published in association with
ACC Publishing Group

CONTENTS

INTRODUCTION

Manners Makyth Man. But they matter more to women. It is an ageless principle that nothing increases a man's attractiveness to his mate as much as his attentiveness to her pleasure. Yet chivalry, embattled by the gender politics of the late twentieth century, has lost its nerve. It's assumed that modern women spoiled the game with their uppity insistence on equality. Social scientists (of both sexes) have issued po-faced tracts on the politics of door-holding. Out in the real world, women have moved on. We know we have better ways of proving ourselves than diving for the doorknob.

A new code of male manners is clearly called for, an intelligent etiquette which allows modern men and women to enjoy their differences without falling into old, patronising patterns. Intelligent etiquette, crucially, takes good manners beyond correct form. It requires men to think things through, to sift the meaningful gesture from the empty politesse. Twenty-first century women don't care, on the whole, if you keep your sword arm free on the High Street. But we love it,

every last post-feminist of us, if you leap to your feet when we enter a room. Why? Because standing denotes a flattering enthusiasm which can scarcely be deemed unacceptable.

Our grandmothers may have been offended by a man in shirt-sleeves, but it's a matter of deep indifference to any sentient woman today if you remove your coat in our presence. Helping us off with ours, on the other hand, is a small personal service carrying the promise of some more interesting frisson. The New Chivalry, in short, is manners with a sexy edge.

Not all of this comes naturally to all men. But unlike a sense of humour, sensitive hands or many other items on the modern woman's wish-list, good manners can be learned. We're not talking stuffed-shirt formality here and there is frankly no breach of etiquette that cannot be filled by a degree of natural charm. It just makes things easier if you know what women want. All we ask is that you make it look like your own idea…

THE NEW CHIVALRY

C hivalry is not dead. It's just been keeping its head down for a bit. And who can blame it when the line between courtliness and condescension has become so blurred?

A damsel, however, need not be in distress to enjoy a considerate gesture.

You're not required to spread your cloak for your mistress's dainty feet, but she won't feel remotely undermined if you help carry the shopping.

Strike the right note and both of you should benefit from your knightly services.

PERSONA

Stress is not sexy. There's a certain kind of man who uses stress as a measure of self-worth ('look how many people want a piece of me') and he's not the man we're after.

Clutching your forehead every time your Blackberry bleeps does not mark you out as an alpha male; it makes you look like a salary monkey on a short leash. Nothing is more impressive, in our time-poor era, than the man with time and attention to spare for others. An air of ease, natural or cultivated, can be a killer advantage.

The easy-mannered man appears to be in control in any situation. This should not be confused with a controlling personality. Our twenty-first century knight knows how to get things done his way without huffing, hectoring or 'do-you-know-who-I-am?' arrogance. He displays the kind of social confidence that puts other people at their ease, and a physical confidence that has nothing to do with macho posturing. You feel that if push came to shove, he could slay dragons or, at the very least, see off a mugger, but pushing and shoving really isn't his style.

Chivalry is, in any case, less action-based these days. Our hero is more likely to throw a conversational lifeline than slash a maiden's bonds (though we can still dream) and he does so gracefully. He is funny, but only rarely at the expense of others, and he convincingly laughs at women's jokes. His impeccable manners are universally applied. He speaks to waiters in the same way that he speaks to his boss, and can relate to children without coming across like a hyperactive reject from Saturday morning television.

Above all, the chivalrous man is a grown-up. He's responsible without being stiff, and he will never embarrass his partner by pulling the grisly 'big kid' routine. He's also been around long enough to know that there's nothing inherently entertaining about throwing bread rolls or stealing traffic cones.

On the other hand, he has an exciting edge about him and a sense of new horizons that is deeply attractive. He looks like a leader, but doesn't pull rank.

Whisper it soft! He makes us feel safe.

PUBLIC MANNERS

Just as men subconsciously prefer women whose waist-to-hip ratio bodes well for childbearing, we recognise that a man who has been 'nicely brought up' will be a better father to any future offspring. Rough and ready Heathcliff types were fine as a teenage fantasy. In the adult world, however, they are an embarrassing liability.

The basics should be automatic. 'Please' and 'thank you' are not optional. Punctuality is important. Perpetually running late does not mark you out as either a very busy (for which read unbelievably important) person or an insouciant maverick. It exposes you as an arrogant incompetent who thinks that his time is more valuable than other people's. Ditto the increasingly common and irritating habit of making and taking endless mobile phone calls, text messages and Blackberry messages while out in company. You may think this makes you looks popular. We think it makes you look like a techno-nerd who can't

organise his life. It also suggests to us that you don't think we are very important.

Respect for elders is non-negotiable, whether the elders in question are your parents, our parents or strangers. We're more impressed when you offer an old person your seat on the bus or train than when you offer it to us (same goes for bag-carrying and door holding etc). Similarly, we love it when you make an effort with children. You don't have to come over like a Blue Peter presenter – just show a genuine interest in their concerns.

'Group manners' are especially important. Some of the nicest men imaginable turn into leery, beery louts when they're out with 'the lads'. Apparently it's to do with bonding and the awful fear that the lads will laugh and point if you don't join in. If, however, we catch sight of you sporting a pair of comedy breasts, we will never, ever want to sleep with you. The choice is yours.

WHAT WOMEN WANT

Yes, actually, we do know how confusing it is for modern men. We're just not sure *why* it's so confusing. We've heard the spluttered arguments about how we want equality one minute and chivalry the next but, darlings, it's really not so difficult. We enjoy being treated like a lady, but we don't want to be patronised. Remember this important distinction and you won't go far wrong.

Most women, these days, recognise that the benefits of feminism will not evaporate like faery gold if a man holds the door for us. The door thing, frankly, is not a deal-breaker. Just don't make a huge production out of it (the loud 'ladies first' exclamation is unnecessary, annoying and reminds us of a halitotic old schoolmaster). We don't expect the full Lady Penelope treatment when we get into your car, but if you let us in first, it will be appreciated.

With revolving doors, by all means observe the gentlemanly convention, but let the woman 'drive' the door at her own speed to avoid the 'bum's rush' effect. Never try to share a compartment – there simply isn't enough room and you'll appear creepy.

Staircases are a no-brainer. Unless you seriously suspect an ambush on the next landing, spare your companion a dog's eye view of your butt (however well toned) and keep a discreet and careful distance from hers as she precedes you.

In the case of lifts, there are territorial issues to consider. If it's 'her' building – home or work – it may look like macho presumption to lunge for the control panel. But if she looks expectantly at you, then it's a signal to take control.

On the street, there are practical reasons – more to do with mud from the wheels of messenger bikes than impromptu sword fights – why a man should walk on the kerbside of the pavement. When this is not easily achieved, we'd rather take our chances than find you dancing around us in awkward circles.

We don't need a guiding hand in the small of the back as we cross the big, dangerous road, but a friendly, shepherding arm may be appreciated in dense and rowdy crowds. We like you to keep a quiet eye on speed and pace, and you should check that we're not having to break into a brisk trot to keep up with you. If you adjust your stride to ours, particularly if we're wearing heels, you will avoid the 'one man and his dog' look. Remember too that often we like to talk as we walk.

There is nothing at all untoward in helping us on with our coats, as long as it's done with confidence and helps rather than hinders us. Just don't – unless the friendship has already progressed well beyond outdoor clothes – start smoothing down the lapels and tucking in our scarves.

The real skill lies in knowing where to stop. Standing up for introductions and goodbyes is basic good manners. Bobbing up and down every time we leave or enter a room soon becomes farcical.

Remember, your main aim is to increase your companion's comfort. If you chance upon a woman who sincerely objects to 'sexist' gestures, you should give in gracefully and without comment. Insist, and the advantage is lost.

COMPLIMENTARY SKILLS

Nothing oils the wheels of a new relationship like a well placed compliment, but nothing, on the other hand, is more clunky than an inappropriate personal remark. Until you know a person well, steer clear of anything that might remotely be construed as sexual.

You can safely admire a woman's jewellery (a particularly good 'opener' as jewels often have an interesting history behind them), but excessive attention to, say, lipstick or shoes, may mark you down as a fetishist.

In social situations with work colleagues, it is particularly important to avoid suggestive remarks. A fail-safe strategy for women of any age or station is to compliment them on their sense of humour. Everybody thinks they have one, and you'll get extra brownie points if you're the first person to notice it.

If the object of your attentions is a mother, then you're home and dry. No woman in the history of the universe has ever objected to glowing praise of her children (overexcited admiration of pretty daughters, however, is to be avoided).

If things are hotting up, it is time to deploy more pointedly personal compliments. Remember that your aim is to establish yourself as a person of rare discernment. This means not going for the obvious target. If the object of your desire is blessed with a spectacular bosom, remark on the delicacy of her wrists. A high-powered businesswoman may prefer to be complimented on her dress than on her whizzy ways with spread sheets. Avoid the obvious pitfalls. Never, ever compliment an obviously overweight woman on her lovely teeth. She might just bite.

As you get to know each other better, it is important to keep the compliments coming. At this stage in the game, general remarks just won't cut the mustard. 'Is that a new dress?' carries a 50 per cent risk of failure, whereas 'I love that neckline' is risk-free, observant, intimate and promotes you, in your partner's eyes, to someone who gives a damn about fashion. Sometimes, though, less is more. The correct response to 'does my bum look big in this?' is not a speech, however sincere, in defence of the larger bottom. A simple 'no' will suffice.

FLIRTING

Good flirts can't help themselves. They flirt with everyone. It's not so much a seduction technique as a form of chivalry; a refined politesse designed to make the other person feel good. Bad flirts have quite the opposite effect. They oppress their companion with heavy-handed come-ons and make them uncomfortable.

Non-sexual flirting is a powerful social and professional tool, but it should never be a transparent attempt at self-advancement. Nor should it come over as a performance. You're not setting out to be charming, you're setting out to be charmed. If you're evidently taken with a new acquaintance, they'll mark you down as a person of good judgement and all kinds of advantages will accrue. But this kind of flirting must be even-handed. If you are obviously more impressed by the younger, prettier or more influential women in the company, you will appear merely predictable. Remember that social/professional flirting is a mind-game. Physical attentions are intrusive and inappropriate; in the workplace they are also illegal. So keep it light and cerebral.

If, on the other hand, you're genuinely looking to 'score' with a member of the opposite sex, you need to narrow your focus. The object of your affections needs to know she's special, so cut back – at least in the opening stages – on compliments to mothers, sisters or best friends. Romantic flirting is all about frisson management – an intimation (and no more) of physical closeness. Holding a look just a heartbeat longer than is usual in everyday polite conversation, a light touch on the hand or arm (not the knee as it makes you look like a lecherous uncle) or an 'accidental' brushing of shoulders or arms are proven means of testing the waters.

If the lady freezes, back off. At this stage, only you and she know of the attempt and you can retire from the field, dignity intact. Persist and you risk a public brush-off, as well as an unhelpful reputation as a sex pest. Your aim is to leave yourself in a position where you can, without embarrassment, try again another time (or with another woman).

Someone, somewhere is aching to respond. Keep your best moves for her.

PUTTING ON THE MOVES

In an ideal world romantic introductions to the woman of your dreams are effected by chance – she drops a hanky, you rescue her kitten, she turns up at your door, dripping wet in a very short towel, helplessly twirling a broken stopcock… you can see where the fantasy often leads.

In the real world of disposable tissues and independent women/kittens, fate is rarely so accommodating. And while it's neither right nor fair in these liberated times, most women expect men to make the first move.

Wine bars, clubs and parties are places where we expect to meet new people and approaches in such environments are fairly low-risk. Conversely, the work place is fraught with problems and approaching women on the street can appear unhinged.

It's corny, but the best way of making contact with a woman you haven't been introduced to is by smiling at her. You can make it a casual 'don't I know you from somewhere?' smile, so long as you don't actually say the words. At this range, it's best to appear cheerful and friendly; 'interesting', poetic types look perilously like weirdos across a crowded room. If she's interested, she'll smile back. It really is that simple.

If she's with friends, try to observe the group dynamics. Are they on a 'girls' night out'? Are men superfluous to requirements or is your 'mark' alert to possibilities? In the latter case, she will almost certainly find a way to detach herself from the crowd, leaving your way clear to open a conversation which should strenuously avoid old chestnuts. The overwhelming odds are that she does go

there often, did not fall from heaven and has not, for one deluded second, ever considered a career in modelling.

Open admiration is fine. Focus on something about her – her laugh, her eyes, not her breasts – and let her know, non-verbally if possible, that you're entranced. If you're out with a group of mates, create a private zone for the two of you, or at least make it clear that your conversation is not for their benefit.

If you're there alone and for no other reason than to pick up girls, invent a better reason fast; it's better to be 'waiting for the others' (oops, you just got a text saying you're in the wrong bar!) than to appear a lone hunter. There's really no harm in establishing some important facts (she'll be just as keen to know your current relationship status), but don't make it sound like you're ticking off a check-list; 'do you live alone?' makes it sound like you're desperate to go back to her place for hot sex this very minute.

At a private party, you can offer to refresh her glass. In pubs or clubs, the etiquette has changed due to the alarming practice of drink-spiking. The correct form now is to ask first and let her watch the barman make the drink. If she declines the offer of a drink, do not take it personally. It doesn't mean she suspects you of having evil designs on her; it just means that she doesn't know you and has opted to play it safe.

It's no longer acceptable – and was always, frankly, on the cheesy side – to have drinks sent over with a note to 'the lovely lady on table nine'.

Similarly, do not be too offended if, after an unbroken run of 'green lights', she doesn't want to give you her phone number. This is a perfectly normal female precaution. Offer yours instead and, if she texts or phones you, respond immediately.

It's just not chivalrous to make a lady sweat.

DATING

Hot dates don't just happen. The perfect romantic interlude consists of equal parts chemistry and strategy. Where to go? What to wear? When to leave?

A clear game plan is something to fall back on when your senses are overloaded and your thoughts are diverted by more interesting possibilities.

This is your chance to sell yourself as a prospective lover and you need to pitch high. Presentation is important, patter helps, but it's the quality of the goods that gets the girl.

With the champagne on ice and the roses in water, it's up to you, the night and the music…

STYLISH ARRANGEMENTS

No woman has ever thought badly of a man for asking her out on a date. Even if she declines the invitation, she will be disinclined, for reasons of personal vanity, to write you off as a desperate loser. So go for it.

You should not be shocked, in these modern times, if the woman does the asking, but it makes sense – particularly if she has made her liking for you obvious – to seize the manly initiative and get in first.

Arranging a first date by text or email may seem casual to the point of cop-out. Sometimes it is the most practical method, but techno-invites need to work harder on 'tone' to maintain the sense of occasion. 'R U UP 4 IT?' lacks romance.

Whether making arrangements face to face or by telephone, come straight to the point. 'Would you like to go out with me sometime?' sounds too much like a sweaty-palmed teenager. 'Would you like to have dinner with me on Thursday?' makes you sound like a man with a plan and leaves room for a graceful get-out (Thursday may be the very night she does Pilates, visits her mother, or washes her hair). If there's a genuine diary clash and she does want to go out with you, she will make this clear. You can then make arrangements for another evening.

If she sounds open to persuasion, throw a casual sounding lifeline, but keep it open ended: 'I'm around next weekend' leaves the ball in her court. 'What about three weeks on Friday?' is overly keen and casts you in the unflattering light of a man with no social life. When in doubt, don't push it. 'Perhaps another time' is a dignified exit strategy.

If your invitation is accepted, you should take charge of the date and arrange where and when to meet. There is nothing nerdy about turning up early for a first date, particularly since your companion will only know about it if she's early too. We'll see it as a good sign if you're there waiting for us – it is distinctly unchivalrous to keep a lady waiting alone in a public place.

If you are unavoidably late – we're talking 'acts of God' here, not a careless attitude of 'things dragging on a bit' at work – call ahead (never text) and let her know. She will want to know if you're talking about minutes or hours – a bald 'I'm running late' provides her with no indication of how long she'll have to wait.

Half an hour is about the maximum amount of time you can expect us to wait; a quarter of an hour is not a capital offence, but still requires apology. If the date is in a restaurant, it's a nice touch to inform the maitre'd of your expected delay. That way we feel less of a lemon and avoid the 'ready to order?' embarrassment. If you do need to cancel the date, as much notice as possible should be given. It's best to cancel by phone; text messaging is only acceptable if this is the only way to get an urgent message through.

There is no excuse, bar hospitalisation or family crisis, for cancelling on the day of the date. Never ever consider a sport-related activity or meeting up with the lads to be an acceptable reason to cancel. It is unforgivable to stand a woman up. A phone call, however abject, does not meet the case; we may not even pick up. A bunch of flowers delivered the next morning may just secure a second chance. But make it a big one.

GROOMED FOR SUCCESS

There is a fine line between grooming and primping. Women appreciate a bit of care and effort going into personal presentation, but you don't want to look like you've spent the entire day fretting about your appearance.

Clothes are less of an issue than you think. Women just don't want to be embarrassed by their date. Unless you are very confident in your fashion choices, it's better to play it safe than to 'make a statement'. Particularly to be avoided are prominent designer logos (you will look like an advert), leather trousers (you will look like a hairdresser) and t-shirts with 'amusing' slogans (you will look, without exception, like a nerd).

Wear something you feel comfortable and confident in, but don't look scruffy. Think your outfit through, and remember, we will look at your shoes. Dress to fit the occasion; wear a shirt and trousers for a smart dinner or the theatre, but jeans and a t-shirt for a casual lunchtime picnic or a few drinks at the pub. We'll remember what you wore on the last date, and the date before that, so try not to wear the same outfit too often.

Hygiene is more of an issue than you think; we'll immediately notice poor standards. There is definitely a time and place for fresh, male sweat, but on a first date you won't have got there. You should, at the very least, have showered within the last twelve hours and it goes without saying that shirts, pants and socks should be clean on for the occasion.

Deodorant is, on the whole, a good plan. A subtle aftershave can also be nice. Go easy, however, on cheaper, highly perfumed 'spray it all over' products; we find the smell of a masculine, freshly soaped neck infinitely sexier. Clean teeth are non-negotiable. Nails should be clean and trimmed, but never evidently manicured. And yes, we know that women do it all the time, but spray-on man-tan is irredeemably tacky.

Hair should not be too carefully coiffed – keep it natural. Sticky-up styles, stiff with hair gel, are tragically pubescent. Highlights, on a man, are plain ridiculous – we're trained to spot the difference between sun-streaks and a salon job; the image of you festooned in tinfoil and discussing shade charts is an instant passion-killer. Also, we cannot say it often enough: bald is not a problem for us. Just cut it very short. Comb-overs, pony-tails and hair transplants fool no-one.

A final word on hair removal. Stubble hurts. We generally don't like goatees, and beards need to be washed more often than hair. As for the recent trend in male waxing, it's entirely up to you, but be aware that if you turn up for the Big Night fresh from an intimate waxing, we will assume that you are not dating your gender of choice.

FIRST DATES

Look on the first date as your interview for the position of boyfriend. You may not, on reflection, wish to take up the post, but you still want to give the best possible account of yourself.

Choose a venue where you will both feel comfortable. A drink at your local with the lads giving you 'thumbs up' signs every time you refill your date's glass shows a lack of sensitivity. On the other hand, the best table at the best restaurant in town may feel like too much investment in a new relationship.

Early evening drinks can be tricky. If you are going to another engagement afterwards, make this clear from the outset or your date will feel that she has failed an audition for dinner. If you are daunted by a three-course conversation, lunch provides all the intimacy you need for flirting, with the advantage of a built-in time limit (if you leave the table panting for more, so much the better).

The purpose of a first date is to get to know one another better. Conversation should be personal, but not confessional. This isn't the time to discuss dreams of world domination or innermost fears. It is precisely the time to make it clear that you are unattached – you cannot be sufficiently unambiguous on this point – but don't feel that you have to offer an explanation for the break-up of your last relationship. Without a modicum of 'background information', your date may assume that you are (a) heartless or (b) heartbroken – neither of these is a good look.

The old rules about not discussing politics or religion are less stringent these days. Most women prefer to know what they're dealing with and, if your passions define your lifestyle, there's no point in fudging it. Talking about money remains incontrovertibly bad form.

Regardless of how the date goes, it is polite to kiss your companion goodbye. Go for the cheek, but linger long enough – assuming this is what you want – for her to slide into a more meaningful embrace. It is no longer necessary to 'see a lady home', but finding her a cab is a gentlemanly touch. If she finds she needs help with directions, that's entirely up to her...

NIGHT OR DAY?

Day dates are a bigger commitment than evening dates. They're longer and involve less alcohol, so you need to feel relaxed and confident in your date's company. Daylight romancing is ideal for a third or fourth date, as it elevates the woman in your life from 'potential squeeze' to 'companion'. This may not seem like a worthwhile promotion to you, but it matters to us.

If the date involves a larger group – say a day at the races or a barbeque – then this is an opportunity to test your dynamic as a couple. Your attitude to your companion should be solicitous but not proprietorial, and physical attentions must be casual and subtle. An arm around the waist or shoulders is fine. There is no objection to hand-holding, except in very dense crowds when it's inconvenient and awkward. Full-on snogging is unpleasant for the company at large and is embarrassing for those involved. Save intimate kisses for the shadows.

The classic evening date is more obviously geared to seduction. This doesn't mean you have to spend the entire night whispering sweet nothings. A carefully chosen movie (avoid shoot-em-ups and car chases) or theatrical production (avoid anything too long/intense) can help set the mood and provides material for stimulating conversation later in the evening.

There's nothing more naturally romantic than a moonlit walk (plan your route in advance). If you're in a city, head for high ground with a panoramic view or for the river – it's what lovers do and there will almost certainly be benches conveniently placed for your greater smooching ease. Also, if the date goes well and leads to more permanent ties, you'll remember it always as 'our bench'. Even if you've never harboured a sentimental thought about street furniture in your life, just play along with this one. It's corny as Kansas in August. But you know what? It works.

ACTIVITY DATES

If you're past the both-talking-at-once stage, but not yet ready to slump in front of the telly with a pizza, an activity date keeps things progressing nicely. You do, however, need to do your research on this one.

Unless you have already established a totally perfect union of hearts and minds, make sure you pick something your companion enjoys a little bit more than you do. This demonstrates a willingness to please and an attractive openness to new ideas.

Above all, the activity date should not be viewed as an opportunity to show off your own prowess at abseiling/bungee jumping and, unless your date is a competitive sports nut, obvious winner/loser situations should be avoided. On the other hand, an activity that invites a modicum of physical contact – ice-skating or kite-flying for example – has clear advantages.

Not that you need to work up a sweat for the date to be a success. Art galleries are a stylish venue for romance. If you are a connoisseur, taking her to see the pictures you love in a gallery you know really well is a delightful way of letting her into 'your' world. If you don't know your arts from your elbow, choose a big, fashionable 'single artist' show. Spend some time swotting up on magazine and internet reviews beforehand. You don't have to be an expert, but you can at least be informed – and if your date sees through it, she will still be charmed by the effort.

Equally, a trip to something or somewhere new to you both will strengthen the delicious sensation of shared experience. Exploring 'hidden quarters' in a city you thought you knew is a curiously intimate excitement, well suited to new love. Plan the day enough to give it shape, but don't slip into tour guide mode – your date will want to feel like she's the main attraction.

Time permitting, an all-day expedition to a castle or country house further afield can be rounded off with a scenic walk and dinner in a country inn (once again, do your research and find a nice one). Who knows? With flattering candlelight and a following wind, you might still be there for breakfast.

TAKING CHARGE

Small attentions have big impact on a date. As our official escort for the occasion, you should – unless you're dating a woman who is plainly annoyed by that sort of thing – take charge of our physical comfort.

Even if we don't normally go in for the whole door-opening, chair-holding routine, we may well find ourselves playing up to it on a date, so it's worth a try. The aim is not to impress us with your impeccable manners (though you undoubtedly will), but to give us the comforting feeling that the world seems less of a hassle when you're around.

By all means help us on with our coat at the end of the evening. It's a small courtesy that makes a woman feel cosseted and cared for. You should hold the coat between the collar and shoulder seam and, once our arms are in the sleeves, lift the coat onto our shoulders. Then – this is the killer move – lift the coat once again to make sure it settles properly on our clothes underneath.

You should perfect the art of hailing a cab with just the right mixture of insouciance and authority. Don't wave at cabs with passengers already ensconced and don't shout 'Taxi!' (cabbies really hate this). Raising your arm at the kerbside should do the job. Tell the driver where you want to go through the front window, hold the back door open and let the lady get in first. If you are in a group, the men should take the fold-down seats, leaving the comfortable banquette for their female companions. At your destination, get out first, leave the back door open for the lady and pay the driver through the window. In mini-cabs, it is polite to sit in the back with your companion. If sharing a taxi to separate destinations, the lady should, if practicable, be dropped off first.

On public transport, let your date board the bus or train before you. If there is a scramble for empty seats, you should, first of all, secure a seat for your companion. It will do you no harm, in your date's eyes, to extend the courtesy to other female passengers before sitting down yourself. If both of you have to stand, it is an opportunity to snake an arm around her waist – no gentleman likes to see a lady jostled. If things are going well, she may initiate some jostling of her own.

While train stations carry a potent erotic charge (we're thinking *Anna Karenina* and *Brief Encounter*), the harsh, fluorescent glare of underground and bus stations is less conducive to romance. If you are planning a goodnight kiss, think ahead and try to find a relatively dimly lit and unexposed corner for your intimate farewells. Supportive cries of 'go for it, mate' from passers-by will not have an encouraging effect on your companion.

MONEY MATTERS

'Going Dutch' on a date is never an option – not even, one imagines, in Holland. Splitting the bill is fair and modern in principle, but in practice you may as well write 'I never ever want to see you again' in letters of fire across the night sky.

At the beginning of a relationship, it is widely accepted that the person who issues the invitation picks up the tab. If you have been invited out by a woman, you might still offer to pay, but concede the privilege if she says 'no' and means it.

If you are old-fashioned and exceptionally generous, you may insist on paying for every aspect of the evening – drinks, taxis, concert tickets etc. There is no loss of face, however, if the lady assumes responsibility for one or more of the minor expenses.

For more established couples, it is fine to take turns – you pay for one date, she pays for the next – so long as things are kept reasonably even. As the relationship shakes down, who pays for what will inevitably be determined by your relative finances.

Money talk should be kept to the minimum. Don't brag or complain about your salary, or fish for information about your companion's financial situation. If you are clearly wealthier than your date, and she still insists on taking turns, you may want to tone down your lifestyle, ensuring she doesn't bankrupt herself by matching your extravagance.

If you genuinely want to treat her, saying something to the effect of 'this is what I love to do, and I love it even more if you're doing it with me' will take the edge off the obligation.

If your date is better placed, financially, than you are, be honest and tell her about your situation; don't stretch yourself beyond your means. If you're out with her friends and they're spending money like it's going out of fashion, bow out before you get involved in paying for expensive meals or rounds of drinks you can't afford.

You can accept the occasional treat with good grace, but avoid the gigolo syndrome as one or both of you will end up feeling resentful.

CALLING IT A DAY

The line 'it's not you, it's me' is possibly the most transparent fib in the social canon. It's also a useful act of kindness and should not be thrown out of court just for being clichéd.

If, by the end of the first date, you have no earthly interest in seeing your companion again, thank her warmly for a lovely evening and leave it at that. It is the height of bad manners to suggest a second date and then run to ground. After two or three dates, you might tell her that spending time with someone as gorgeous as she is has made you realise that you're just not ready for a relationship right now, and that you respect her too much not to be honest with her.

Dumping is best done face to face or, at the very least, by phone. Texting is juvenile and emails may be angrily forwarded on to her entire address book for comment. If the penny fails to drop on the first attempt, you must persevere. Don't leave it to us to figure out that, five unanswered phone calls and ten text messages later, you're just not that interested. Nor should mutual friends be presumed upon to break the bad news.

If you're the one who has been dumped, you are perfectly entitled to ask for a reason. Just don't press too hard for the truth. If your date scrupulously avoids any mention of future meetings, keeps giving excuses as to why she can't meet or wants to invite friends along to 'make up a crowd', you should take the hint without bargaining or begging. In the nicest possible way, lead her to believe that she only just beat you to the finishing line and part on pleasant terms. 'Let's stay friends' is not a binding contract.

TAKING IT FURTHER

Playing it cool always looks great in movies. Bond girls are remarkably accommodating about 007's slippery habits – he shrugs them off like last night's tuxedo and charges off to save the civilised world, leaving an orderly queue of women panting for his return.

Real women in real life need a bit more to work with. If you want to see them after the first date, you must call them the day after. Whatever happens, no matter how busy you are, you have to make that call.

If you're really keen, call your date when you get home and thank her for a lovely evening but (and this is where the psychology comes in) don't finalise details of your next meeting at this stage. You may have decided, in the course of the date, that you want to see each other again, but leave it a day or so before arranging the specifics of your next meeting. It's a courtly charade guaranteed to keep the excitement going.

Nobody needs more than three dates to make up their mind about a person. If you haven't tried to kiss her by the third date, your companion will assume that you're out of the game. After three dates, you can also safely be said to be 'seeing someone' (not necessarily exclusively at this stage). Six dates or more and it's definitely time to decide whether you're going to take things further or call it a day.

If you want it to be an exclusive relationship, you must say so in words. So much the better if you make a small romantic ceremony of it with a special meal, flowers or head-spinning kiss. Graduating from 'date' to 'boyfriend' is a significant landmark in a relationship and you should try not to flinch, flush or react with anything other than a delighted smile when you are introduced as such.

If you feel self-conscious about saying 'this is my girlfriend', then you must make it clear by the tone of your voice (confident) and body language (into her) that you are proud to be with her. You might also try asking her if she minds the label of girlfriend – a roundabout way of expressing your own unease. There's a very good chance that she really won't mind one bit.

SEDUCTION

The 'bold seducer' has fallen out of fashion. There's just not the demand, in a post-feminist world, for mustachio-twirling rogues with designs on a maiden's honour. Modern seduction is a distinctly less goal-orientated pursuit, more about pleasing a woman than storming her defences.

Sexual etiquette is constantly evolving; while the process of persuasion may have shortened somewhat, twenty-first century women expect their choices to be respected.

Responsibility is as sexy as romance. Together, they're irresistible.

THE FOOD OF LOVE

'I placed the shell on the edge of her lips,' wrote Casanova, *'and after a good deal of laughing, she sucked in the oyster...'*

The daddy of all lovers, it turns out, was spot-on with his performance-enhancing breakfast of 50 oysters; the suggestive bivalves are rich in testosterone-producing zinc. It's a fair bet, however, that her laughing contributed as much to Casanova's success as the shellfish. You simply cannot, in a post-modern universe, set out a casual 'seduction supper' of oysters, asparagus ('ooh Signor Casanova, what a long one!') and ripe figs with a straight face. If you are sure that your date will see the joke, by all means ham it up. If not, you must choose your aphrodisiacs sparingly. Either way, you should be confident about how to prepare and consume the 'classics' of seduction cuisine. Remember, however, that many such foodstuffs are an acquired taste. It's impolite to force things on a lady that she doesn't like.

OYSTERS
Eating oysters only when there is an 'R' in the month means eating them when the sea is coldest. Modern refrigeration has obviated the need for excessive caution on this front, but a bad oyster is thoroughly unromantic. A good oyster smells clean and seasidey, with no hint of fishiness. Beware of shrivelled, blackish or cloudy flesh; the oyster should be translucent grey or brown with a white muscle.

Present the oysters shucked (i.e. detached) but in the shell. A really fresh specimen will 'wince' at the addition of lemon juice; but only a sadist would point this out to his companion. The correct way to eat an oyster is to knock it back in one. Grasp the shell by its sides, look for a suitable 'launch pad' on the rim, tip your head back and slide the slippery customer in. Savour for a moment in the mouth, but do not chew. Slurp down the salty liquor remaining in the shell – it's all part of the treat.

Champagne is a glamorous accompaniment, but any crisp, white wine – say a Muscadet or Sancerre – goes well with oysters. For those of the rugged persuasion, Guinness is a perfectly stylish alternative.

CAVIAR
Caviar is undeniably flash, but fun if you know what you're doing. Theatrical types can taste the caviar off their hand (spoon a small amount into the hollow between thumb and first finger). It's not mere affectation as 'off' roe will smell on contact with flesh. Fresh caviar should never taste salty. Once you're satisfied with the quality (and it would be a little embarrassing if, as the host, you are not), use your plate and keep servings small – no more than 30 grams per person.

Unfinished caviar should be removed from the tin and refrigerated in a champagne flute. It should always, however, be eaten at room temperature. Accompaniments such as sour cream and onion or chopped egg, though scorned by purists, are useful for eking out a potentially ruinous treat.

ASPARAGUS
Asparagus is in season in May. Snap off its woody ends and serve simply steamed with butter or hollandaise sauce. Pick up by the root end and eat with your fingers (except when asparagus is served as a vegetable with a meal, when you should use a knife and fork).

FRUIT
Figs have long been associated with sex and female fertility because of their suggestive shape and colouring. The correct way to eat figs is sliced into quarters, but you can just go for it and take a bite. When eating strawberries, hold by the hull and bite straight in. Rakish types may wish to feed the fruit (with champagne or chocolate for dipping) to their guest. Do not be offended if she giggles.

CHOCOLATE
Everything they say about chocolate is true. Mood lifting substances – serotonin and phenylethylamine – are released by the brain when we're experiencing feelings of love and passion, and when we're eating chocolate. The notable exception is chocolate body paint/novelties shaped like secondary sexual characteristics, which have a profoundly depressing effect on the female psyche.

DINING OUT

A dinner date is a chance to impress your dining partner with your *savoir faire*, not an opportunity to impose your own tastes upon her. It is no longer de rigueur, even in the smartest restaurants, for the gentleman to order for the lady. If you know the cuisine well and we do not, we may like to be guided by you, but we are quite able to communicate our wishes to the waiter.

It's particularly important to reserve your table at the weekend and, if you're planning to make a lingering, romantic night of it, make sure the restaurant doesn't operate a 'second sitting' policy. If there is a 'best table' in the restaurant, you could put in a bid by saying it's a special occasion.

If you are meeting at the restaurant, the gentleman should arrive first; check that the table is satisfactory and leave the 'best' chair – traditionally the one facing into the room – for the lady.

Steer clear of foodstuffs that you can't control. Spaghetti is notoriously wilful, lobster needs a man to show it who is boss (start with the tail-meat then crack those claws like an East End gangster). The single worst solecism that you can commit *à table* is to comment on the table manners of others. This does not mean that if your dining companion drinks from the fingerbowl you have to return the toast with yours. By all means lead by example. Just don't go on about it.

Take care with foods you can't pronounce. Unless your French/Italian/Bengali is up to scratch, it is much better to point at the item on the menu than risk a muffled titter from the waiter. If you have absolutely no idea what the proposed delicacy is, ask the waiter to tell you 'a bit more' about the preparation of the dish.

A date isn't the time to demonstrate your competitive eating skills. Never comment on your partner's appetite. If we're on a diet, fielding allergies, or just plain faddy, we will not appreciate your efforts to tempt us from our chosen regime. Should you, romantically, decide to share a pudding, remember it is not a race to the finish.

Lovingly feeding each other tasty morsels is (just) admissible in low lighting, but it makes gruesome viewing. Mutual finger-licking must be kept for the privacy of home. The advice of fellow diners to 'get a room' will not be welcomed by your date.

WINE AND ROSES

Navigating the wine list is a basic social skill. The 'red for meat and white for fish/poultry' mantra is a very useful rule of thumb, but it's not a hanging offence to go off-piste. Take the time to swot up and discover for yourself which wines go with different foods. Make sure you're clued-up on prices – you don't want your newly found expertise to bankrupt you. Should you wish to impress on a budget, make a study of New World wines – they are perfectly smart and considerably cheaper.

There is absolutely no shame – particularly when patronising fancier establishments – in asking the sommelier for advice, but keep an eye on the prices of his favoured vintages. It's also better to order by bin number or point at your selection on the wine list than to attempt pronunciation in an unfamiliar language.

Wine must be tasted with maximum confidence and minimum fuss. Swishing and gargling are pointless and embarrassing to watch. A quick sniff and sip will tell you all you need to know. Acknowledge your acceptance with a friendly nod to the waiter, or say 'that's fine, thanks'. If the wine is 'corked' (or 'off'), it will have a distinctive dish-clothy odour. Bits of cork or sediment in the wine are not a reason to send it back and you're only given

the cork to inspect the information, so never sniff it. Remember too that screw tops are no longer the sign of a cheap bottle.

If you think something is amiss, now is the time to say so. You cannot complain when you're half way down the bottle. If the wine you've chosen is in good condition but not to your liking, there's not a whole lot you can do about it. Unless you are well informed enough to argue the toss with the sommelier over a particular vintage, it's good form to stand by your choice – or pay for another bottle. There are no extra points for being difficult.

Fill your companion's glass first. Stop when you reach the widest part of the 'tulip'; never overfill it. A brimming glass suggests not only a lack of *savoir faire*, but also the unchivalrous desire to get the lady legless.

It is, of course, polite to check that she approves your choice of wine. If she turns out to be a bit of a wine buff, it's always wise to defer to her judgement. If, on the other hand, she wants white wine or, for that matter, a piña colada with her sirloin, order it without huffing or fussing. The wine waiter may be less than impressed, but who do you want to take home – the woman or the waiter?

DRINKS AT HOME

There is a sacramental quality to wine which beer/lager/cocktails fail to deliver. Sharing a bottle is one of the ceremonies of romance; sharing a special bottle is as much, for women at least, about emotional investment as it is about the oenophile experience.

Don't let the moment slip through your fingers by banging on about the depth and deliciousness of the wine when you could more usefully be concentrating on our own fine qualities. The extra respect you accord the wine (decanter for red or ice bucket for white) will make it sufficiently (and flatteringly) clear you're pushing the boat out.

Choosing the right glass for the right wine will mark you out as a man who cares more about getting things right than getting drunk. Hearty reds need a large-bowled glass to release the bouquets (aromas). A narrower bowl delivers whites to the appropriate taste receptors to combat acidity. This, unless you're really stuck for conversation, is not something you need to pass on. You're aiming to present yourself as a casual aficionado, rather than a desperate geek.

You might, however, strike a flirty note by testing the theory that the old-fashioned champagne coupe – bowl-shaped and less efficient than a 'flute' since they let the carbon dioxide (fizz) dissipate – was modelled on the shape of Marie Antoinette's bosom. There is also potential for a double whammy here as champagne is a perennially glamorous treat.

Of course, on more casual occasions, it's just enough to have a decent bottle of red and a chilled white on hand. Stock up, for impromptu visits, with impressive wines sold as 'end-of-bin bargains', but don't hoard them for long; often they're cheap because they're near the end of their shelf-life.

Cocktails can be fun if you've got the right paraphernalia, but avoid girly excess. A simple margarita or mojito, assembled from high quality ingredients, is far classier than day-glo concoctions involving umbrellas.

Drinks with amusingly sexual or provocative names (anything long, slow or – God help us – up against the wall) are to be avoided. They rarely live up to their promise.

GOOD TALK

Women like to talk more – or at least talk *about* more – than men. This can make conversation between the sexes tricky. Men, on the whole, are interested in the general exchange of information. Women – not all women, but enough women – will sift each sentence for subtext.

You say: 'That restaurant is always full of screaming kids.'

We hear: 'On no account get emotionally attached to me as I am a dyed-in-the-wool commitment-phobe who will never, ever, want to settle down and have babies with you.'

You say: 'That dress really shows off your figure.'

We hear: 'Dear God! What kind of whorish get-up is she wearing?'

And so it goes on...

It's nobody's fault; it's really just the way women are programmed. And it's also why eye contact is crucial in any kind of verbal seduction. To make us feel comfortable while we chat, your eyes need to beam full approval. If it's clear from your reactions that you are also listening to what we are actually saying, then it's an incalculable bonus.

What we say will, in all probability, be on the abstract side – hopes/dreams/interests/fears. You will, naturally, wish to counter this talk with accounts of contracts won and penalties scored. You will assume that, because we keep on asking questions (in the dogged hope of establishing emotional contact), we are enthralled by everything you say. If we fancy you, we won't terribly mind. If, on the other hand, that deal has yet to be clinched, there are certain steps you can take to turn conversation to your advantage.

First, you need to set a timer in your head. If you have been talking about yourself for more than ten minutes, then it's time to switch roles and ask some interested questions about your companion.

Secondly, you need to listen to the answers. Listening well means remembering what we say and then using this information at a later juncture. Watch closely to see which subjects engage and animate us the most and keep these topics well shuffled and ready to play. Find a way of making it clear that you admire our ideas and opinions just as much as our décolletage (talking to our face, not our chest, is the ideal starting point).

Should you run into an emotional/ideological impasse, laughter is your 'get out of jail free' card. Just don't make every joke an evasion technique. In fact, go easy on jokes *per se*. Aim for more female-friendly observational humour whenever possible.

Don't be afraid of short natural lulls. There's nothing like a pause in conversation – no longer than a heartbeat – to crank up the erotic charge, particularly if accompanied by some meaningful eye contact. Too much silent staring, however, will scare us and if you overdo the 'companionable silence' at the beginning of the relationship we assume you are bored.

Remember, a woman in love will forgive just about anything you say. It's what you don't say that spooks us.

BAD HABITS

Nobody's perfect and not all bad habits are deal-breakers. That said, any man honing his seduction skills will do well to avoid:

ARROGANCE

The dangerous delusion that your needs, desires or opinions are, without exception, more important than the next man's is the number one turn-off for women. Arrogance should never be confused with confidence. If you're boasting to impress us, it is likely to have the opposite effect. Ladies know that quality is discreet. We wouldn't pick a handbag that shouts too hard and we won't pick you.

TANTRUMS

Losing your temper – particularly in public – shows a worrying lack of self control. Shouting at people you don't know and who are not in a position to shout back (such as waiting staff, juniors etc.) is particularly unattractive, as is any degree of physical aggression.

BEING DRUNK

Drink is a great disinhibitor. The snag is that it only disinhibits the drinker. Once you are disinhibited to the point of declaring your love for barmaids/bus drivers/lampposts, we will be less than receptive to any more *ad feminam* advances. If getting oiled is part of the night's fun, gauge it carefully so you are never drunker than we are. We do not want to be responsible for getting you home.

SMOKING

If you smoke and we don't, we will mind the smell. We'll mind it on your clothes and hair and we'll mind it even more on ours. Crucially, we will never want to slip between your malodorous sheets.

PATRONISING BEHAVIOUR

Modern women do not take well to being 'corrected' in their dress, speech or opinions. You may see yourself as Pygmalion. We just see the pig.

GENTLEMANLY BEHAVIOUR

There is a very fine line between defending a lady's honour and coming on like a caveman. If another man tries to flirt with us when we are out with you, take it as a compliment the first time. If he persists, then let him know, in affable fashion, that you are our escort for the evening. If all else fails, ask him, calmly and politely, to leave.

If we are harassed or insulted by a drunk, let us handle it in our own way (if we want to). If we are upset or if the threat is physical, step in and remove us from the situation. Ignore any invitation or impulse to fight. Going toe-to-toe in a Neanderthal rutting display will not improve matters. Your priority is to look after our immediate interests, not our honour and certainly not your pride, and to prevent an embarrassing situation from getting worse.

If our own behaviour is less than ladylike, the minimum fuss rule still applies. Informing us bluntly that we have had far too much to drink is unlikely to go down well and may prove something of an 'own goal'; it is not unknown for ladies in this situation to assert their feminist right to drink more.

Depending on your companion's degree of awareness, you might offer to get her a glass of water or discreetly substitute her next drink for a mixer (at this stage in the proceedings a gin and tonic without the gin is a thoughtful and forgivable deception).

If all else fails, call it a night. Plead an early start, an approaching hurricane – anything but how embarrassingly drunk and out of control she is. Keep it light or you could seem overly controlling and patronising. Make sure you see her home safely, no matter how great a detour it involves.

It goes without saying that no gentleman will ever take advantage of a drunk woman. The real test of chivalry is your reaction the morning after. Your companion will invariably be embarrassed and may, in a desperate act of self-loathing, beg for details.

If you want to see her again (and are not, as a general rule, concerned about her level of drinking), affect breezy amnesia with regard to the entire incident. She won't be fooled, but she'll be awfully grateful.

BACHELOR PAD

Your living environment says more than your clothes about the person you are (or want to be). If you're keen to step up to the next stage of a relationship, your home will, sooner or later, come under scrutiny. If you live with your mother, this is the time to declare it. If you live on your own, or with flatmates, make an effort for the 'first viewing'.

Before you invite the girl of your dreams over, conduct a frank, detailed review of your living conditions. 'Clean' is a rigorously subjective term; that forgivingly hazy effect on the bathroom mirror may look alarmingly like filth to feminine eyes. Lavatories, you will find, are a particular point of concern. Most modern women aren't too exercised about the whole loo seat up/loo seat down debate, but do expect said loo to be flushed after use.

Signs of excessive fastidiousness can also be off-putting. As ever, it's a matter of balance. Classifying CDs by musical genre is logical, classifying CDs by colour is scary. Should we open your kitchen cupboard and find food tins ranked by height with their labels facing

outward we will assume you are a serial killer and run shrieking into the street.

The aim is to present your home as an adult environment. Evident over-reliance on flashy games consoles might suggest arrested development and underemployment. Pornography of any persuasion will not be tolerated by a potential girlfriend and must be removed.

Certain things, however, will please a female visitor. A few family photos argue for a balanced family background and pictures taken while travelling hint at wide horizons. Art posters (framed) are a good bet, but avoid the usual suspects – even Mme Monet, one presumes, got tired of those damned poppies – and select prints from an exhibition that you may feasibly have visited.

A nod to modern, healthy living – fresh fruit, flourishing houseplants – will encourage us. Add a stack of clean white towels in the bathroom – more than you ever dreamed necessary – and the scene is set for seduction.

INVITING US OVER

Entertaining us at home gives a modern, metrosexual gloss to the old-fashioned (i.e. reassuring) notion of man-as-provider. If you are a whizz in the kitchen, this is your chance to show off. If you're not a confident cook, there's no need for panic; you can buy in starters and pudding from a good deli and follow a simple recipe for the main course. If you're still anxious, try roasting a chicken – it couldn't be simpler and the smell alone conjures instant domestic competence.

Whatever you choose to cook, it must be in the oven or prepped and ready to cook by the time we arrive. The first reason for this is basic good manners – you will want to sit down and talk to us rather than be caught running around with your pinny on fire. The second reason is that girls snoop. We just can't help it. Half the time we don't even

know we're doing it. But left to chat amongst ourself while you faff about in the kitchen, we will extract or extrapolate more personal info about you than MI5.

In the time it takes you to spin a salad we will, without so much as opening a drawer, have found out everything, from your relationship with your mother to the state of your bank balance and when you last had sex. This forensic process is made much easier if you're careless enough to leave your flatmates lying about the house, but the careful host will have taken care of this well in advance.

Your best bet is simply to contain us. Clearly, a request for the bathroom cannot be denied, but there is no need to provide a tour of the house. This is in any case best avoided, since in an erotically promising atmosphere, there is no possible way of saying 'and this is the bedroom' without sounding like you're on a hair-trigger for 'the off'.

Soft lighting/music indubitably help things along, but you want to go easy on the whole candle-lighting, chair-adjusting thing or you will come across like a nervous waiter. After dinner, if you are scorchingly sensitive to cliché, you may wish to avoid the move to the sofa. Or you could make an ironic play of it. Or – and this is the option most favoured by women – you can (a) get over yourself and (b) get on with it.

Unless your dinner guest has arrived clutching an overnight bag, you should, at some point, offer her the option of calling for a taxi. Make this sound considerate – the action of a man

remembering his manners, rather than the action of man desperate to catch the end of the match on Sky Sports.

If we decide to stay over, the casual offer of a clean t-shirt to sleep in can strike a sweetly un-presumptuous note (if nothing else, we'll be grateful for something to put on while stumbling to the bathroom in the morning).

Breakfast – at least fresh coffee, juice and toast – is part of the deal. And if you have to leave for work early, there should be no sense that you're rushing us out too. Put your trust in the arcane feminine code of honour that forbids snooping in an empty house – it's just too tacky, and where's the forensic challenge? In any case you really should, by now, know us well enough.

IN THE BEDROOM

No woman ever wants to be bounced into a den of iniquity. Satin sheets, overhead mirrors etc. are the stuff of adolescent fantasy and give grown women the creeps. Duvet covers and curtains in football team colours are barely more encouraging and should be binned along with Formula 1 posters, girlie mags (most particularly in the vicinity of the bed), alarm clocks shaped like baseballs and any other objects that loudly scream 'arrested adolescence'.

It's sometimes thought that an old teddy bear, prominently positioned, will provoke warm, fuzzy feelings in female visitors. This is the first, dangerous step into the moral descent which begins with soft toys and toe-curling pronouncements ('Teddy says he likes you') and ends with adult men uttering the dreaded words 'I'm just a Big Kid, really'. It should, by now, be most abundantly clear that women, while often fond of children and their whimsical ways, have no desire to wake up next to one.

It goes without saying that bed linen should be fresh and clean. Make sure there are plenty of pillows (of recent vintage) and ironed pillow cases may impress us further. The bed should be well made and look enticing enough for us to want to jump in.

Lighting is probably more important to girls than to boys and should therefore be given close attention. If all you have is an overhead bulb and a spotlight for reading, consider the flattering glow of candlelight. Yes, candles are on the feminine side, but we will understand that you are doing it just for us. We will also understand that scented candles are, for most men, a bridge too far.

Books on the bedside table bespeak a life of the mind, but should be carefully edited. Fantasy and sci-fi aren't encouraging choices for men over the age of consent and marks will be deducted for any novel which was first a film. It doesn't strictly matter if you've read them or not; after all, your guest has not come for a literary quiz.

A book of poetry, however (something classy and unmushy – Auden, perhaps, or Larkin) may be just the thing for the afterglow...

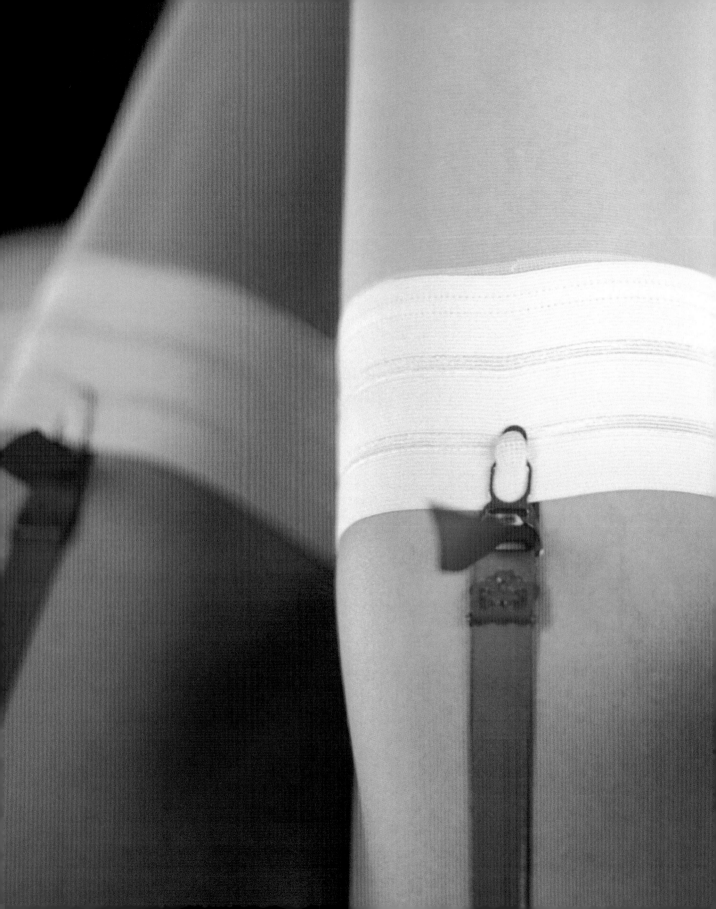

SEDUCTION AND SEX

You will have read, in repeated media surveys, that women prefer chocolate to sex. This is not true. It's just that you know where you are with a KitKat. Trust is as vital as lust. Our decision to sleep with a man will be based largely on whether we feel comfortable with him. We will not feel comfortable with him if he is behaving like a sprinter limbering up for the 100-metre dash.

A relaxed, unhurried manner will put us at our ease. This may take a bit of stage-managing – turning off your phone, paying off flatmates to stay out etc. If we have kicked off our shoes and declined the offer of a taxi home, it's a very good sign, but nothing should be taken for granted. Staying after midnight does not necessarily mean we want to proceed straight to bed without passing 'Go'.

Signals, at this stage in the game, will be largely non-verbal but, if you're in any doubt, it is entirely appropriate to ask us in plain (not coarse) language whether we're comfortable about staying the night. Any embarrassment we might feel about such a direct approach will be offset by admiration at the fact that you are mature enough to discuss the situation.

It is pointless to say that when push, as it were, comes to shove, women don't like to be rushed (some like it just fine), but try to match your pace to ours and remember that one green light doesn't mean a straight run home. Be aware, too, that if anything is going to tauten every nerve and sinew in our body it is a man instructing us to relax.

No matter how much it flies in the face of received male wisdom, no matter how much you want it to mean something else, 'No' always – and at any point in the proceedings – means 'No'. Begging, pleading or sulking in the face of a late refusal is ungentlemanly. Try not to take it personally (difficult in the circumstances but remember that sex is a hugely complicated business; it may indeed be something you said or did, or it may be something entirely unrelated). Be nice about it. There is nothing more tantalising than a man who takes rejection well.

In the happy event that the evening concludes exactly as you hoped, pillow talk never goes amiss. Resist the urge to turn onto your face and snore, and reflect, with satisfaction, that when everything is right, 'Yes' means 'Yes Yes Yes!'

OUT AND ABOUT

Naturally, you will wish to impress your consort with your social *savoir faire*. There is nothing more attractive than the man who knows how to handle himself in every situation.

The truly savvy individual is a life-enhancer, commanding as much affection as respect. In awkward situations, he smooths the path for his companions and especially for his partner.

Whether you're hosting a black-tie dinner, or facing the black run at Klosters, knowing the correct form (and when to depart from it) will give you confidence to step up to the mark.

SHOPPING

There is no escape. Resistance is useless. If you thought that by arranging sports fixtures, signing up for voluntary work or punching yourself repeatedly in the eye, you could avoid the hell that is Saturday Shopping With The Girlfriend, you were wrong. Your only recourse is to formulate a game plan and stick to it.

Do not think of opening proceedings with the phrase 'but what is it you actually need?'. Whereas men approach shopping on a strictly need-to-buy basis, women are genetically disposed to browse. Attempts to streamline the process will inevitably lead to the classic high street stand-off, where Man stomps off to the nearest pub and Woman takes twice as long over her purchases out of principle.

In the small matter of clothes shopping, a gentleman will take his partner's opinion into account when making his fashion choices. You may feel you have all the clothes you need, but if your partner has identified areas of concern, it's best to go along with the plan. 'But darling, I've already got trousers' is insufficient argument against a new pair and

selecting the cheapest item on offer fools no-one. As a rule of thumb, clothes shopping with a woman costs three times as much as clothes shopping alone. For reasons which may never become clear, the extra cost, time and effort will be 'worth it'.

Similarly, when shopping for women's clothes, accept as a matter of good faith that there are important differences, discernible only to the female eye, in a line-up of black, short-sleeved t-shirts. Several of these will make us look unaccountably fat, but this is not, repeat not, an area in which you should attempt to second-guess our judgement. Nor should you point to a younger, thinner woman in the shop and suggest we emulate her style. Much better to seize on one of the identical looking garments and pronounce it the sexiest thing you ever saw in your life (it helps, too, if you put the newspaper down while delivering your opinion). This method is both time efficient and pragmatic as your girlfriend will doubtless wish to live up to the promise of her new purchase – a 'win-win' situation with the happy potential for two entirely satisfied customers.

RESTAURANT RULES

It's easy to impress women in the movies. For a start, the amiable yet discriminating hero invariably has a top-notch neighbourhood restaurant where he can drop in at any hour and be welcomed like a returning son. In real life, eating out requires planning. Booking ahead lacks raffish spontaneity, but so does pleading when the restaurant is full.

You will know, by now, what our food preferences are and you should observe them. There's no point taking a vegetarian out for a celebration meal to a steakhouse. Even if your other half is a committed carnivore, she is unlikely to enjoy those establishments where braying City Boys tuck into bizarrely expensive offal as a kind of macho dare.

Never allow your table manners to let you down. Table settings, however elaborate, are logical and therefore congenial to the masculine psyche. Start from the outside and work in. Do not hold your knife like a pencil, nor your fork like a shovel. Push your spoon away from you while eating soup, return your cutlery to the centre of the plate when you're finished and you really can't go far wrong. Chopsticks are a different matter. Until you're confident in their use (practice at home with individual baked beans) stick to the flatware you know.

Arriving early gives you a chance to study the menu beforehand, so you can give your full attention to your partner when she arrives. It also means you get to edit the wine list for a selection of wallet-appropriate vintages, thus avoiding the embarrassing 'this looks nice… ah, maybe not' moment.

It is never appropriate, however, to steer your companion's food choices away from the expensive end of the menu, or to try and push her into eating something just because you like it and think that she should try it.

Of course there is no necessity, in an established relationship, for the man to pay for every meal out (taking turns shows more confidence in the relationship than splitting the cost each time). If you are paying, however, you should do so discreetly. Check the bill without disrupting conversation. Wincing at the total, clutching your forehead or cracking jokes about washing dishes will shatter your sophisticated image.

BARS

Bar behaviour says a lot about a man. The confident character registers his place in the queue with a 'when you're ready' nod to the bar staff, and waits his turn without shouldering, huffing or puffing. Venting your frustration on those around you if you don't get served straight away veers dangerously close to 'do you know who I am?' arrogance and is all too easily slapped down ('nope, don't know, don't care').

In a bar with table service, it is customary to tip the staff if there is no service charge already included. If you are 'hosting' the table and footing the bill – rather than going round for round with your companions – you should settle the tip at the end of the evening when you pay. The going rate is 10 per cent and it should be remembered that bar staff are frequently dependent on tips to make up their wages. For bar staff, the convention is to offer a drink (or the price of a drink) rather than cash.

If you are in a group and everyone is buying drinks, remember when it's your round and ask everyone what they'd like before you're reminded that it's your turn. Your girlfriend will probably want to stand her own rounds, but if you're socialising with a circle of friends you know well and she has barely met, you might consider stepping in to cover her round. If she insists on paying, be sure to return the compliment when you're out with her friends.

Flirting with bar or table staff when you're accompanied by your partner is bad form (to be honest, it's fairly tragic at any time). Flirting with other female customers at the bar, while your partner looks on or waits (im)patiently at a table, is unforgivable.

Unlike a night out with the lads, a drink with your girlfriend is not a race to the finish line. Women tend, on the whole , to drink less than men and do not like to be cajoled or bullied into drinking more. Don't let us know you're waiting for us – we drink more slowly than you.

If we don't drink at all, this should not be treated as any kind of dampener on the occasion. A grown up relationship does not depend on either party getting drunk to end the evening well.

CLUBS

NIGHTCLUBS

The great advantage of going to a club with a woman, as opposed to going to a club to *find* a woman, is that it's a whole lot easier to get in. Male-only groups are viewed differently to a happy couple.

Relieved of the onus of blagging the door staff, you don't want to blow it by appearing cocky or combative. It is more than probable that yes, the bouncer has seen a Black Belt in judo before and no, he wasn't looking at your girlfriend funny.

The disadvantage of going to a club with a woman is that since these establishments are generally the preserve of singles, other men will doubtless home in on her charms. There is absolutely no point in getting stroppy about this, not least because the admiring onlooker will probably be there with a gang of mates from the Bare Knuckle Fighting Association and the music will be too loud for your devastating Oscar Wilde put downs to take effect. Try to view compliments to your girlfriend, however basic, as a reflection of your own good taste.

While you may, in your bachelor days, have seen dancing as a necessary evil to place you within pulling distance of attractive women, your girlfriend will not want to spend the evening nursing a pint along the wall. Nor will she care to dance on her own.

If you are not confident in your choreography, it is best to stick to one or two safe and unambitious moves. It may be, of course, that your confidence on the dance floor improves dramatically as the night wears on, but it's nonetheless a good idea to keep checking your partner's reaction. Avoid dancing with girls you don't know, and keep a respectable distance from female friends – the dance floor can all too easily make innocent fun seem like a flirty move.

VIP areas are invariably disappointing. The small triumph of breezing beyond the red rope must be weighed against the (more likely) scenario of forcible ejection. It's just not worth the humiliation.

PRIVATE MEMBERS' CLUBS

Membership of a private club is a stylish addition to the metropolitan lifestyle. Much kudos will accrue from being a member of certain establishments but beware – bragging about it will soon make you look like a social climber.

When issuing invitations to your private club, you should always refer to the establishment by name rather than 'my club', a transparently self-aggrandising term which makes you sound pompous and way above your station. Be conscious of the feminist sensibilities of your girlfriend should your club be a male-only establishment. Tact and diplomacy may temper her wounded pride – a swanky night out will certainly compensate.

As you will need to sign your guests in, it is important that you arrive first and that your guests know where in the club to find you. You can tell reception that you are expecting visitors and where you will be. It is highly embarrassing and bad form for 'unclaimed guests' – particularly unaccompanied females – to be left waiting in the foyer. They won't wait long.

CASINOS

The smarter kind of casino is usually members only. It is sometimes possible to pay an on-the-spot joining fee but, if your aim is to impress your consort, this can seem more desperate than debonair.

The dress code in casinos is fairly rigid – collar and tie, no jeans, no trainers (except in Las Vegas where you can wear your lucky chicken suit if you feel it helps). The door is not the place to debate the pointlessness of dressing up to lose your shirt.

It is not considered condescending for a gentleman to give his female companion some money to gamble with. If it is her first time, you should explain how the various table games work and direct her away from any games where serious play is taking place. If it is your first time in a casino, you should watch, without comment, until you have picked up the rules.

Should you become absorbed in a long and drawn-out game, make sure your guest isn't feeling neglected. Nor should you give full rein to your gambling demons, betting more than you can afford, pounding the table when your number fails to come up, or grasping co-players by the lapels when they attempt to leave the table. Quit while you're ahead; 'loser' has such an unromantic ring.

FORMAL DINNERS

A formal dinner does what it says on the tin. It's an occasion where form, however archaic, must be observed. The Army, Inns of Court, certain City institutions and the older universities each build their own eccentricities into the ritual.

The well-mannered escort will brief his partner thoroughly on dress-code, proceedings and protocol before the event. If you're attending the dinner as a guest and are unfamiliar with the rules, it is better to ask beforehand than to risk a solecism. Committed class warriors, anarchists and individualists are probably better off staying at home.

On going in to table, all women should be seated before the men (an exception may be made at certain university colleges with a distinguished history of feminism where this is deemed a chauvinist outrage). The pulling out/pushing in of ladies' chairs is traditionally the man's responsibility and should be executed with minimum fuss and flourish.

Table manners are tuned up a gear at formal dinners. This is not the time to sneak titbits from your partner's plate or scramble to help yourself from serving dishes. Dishes should be passed and held for ladies on either side of you before you serve yourself.

Eyebrows will be raised if you help yourself to wine without checking others' glasses first, or if you neck your drink. Pace yourself and match your speed to the others at your table.

Conversation at the table should also be equally distributed. If you find yourself seated between a rose and a thorn, you must persevere with your pricklier neighbour for at least one of the courses; if you discuss

Gross National Products of emergent nations throughout the guinea fowl and duchesse potatoes, then you are free to whoop it up with a prettier woman at dessert. There is, of course, no compunction to flirt with your neighbours but time, on these sometimes tedious occasions, goes a lot faster if you set out to be charming.

A toast – most usually the Loyal Toast – is likely to be proposed at the end of the dinner. The drill here is simple and unvaried; if the National Anthem is played first, you stand for the music, leaving your champagne on the table. You then raise your glass for the toast ('The Queen!'), take a sip (not a swig) and sit down. It is better to follow a beat behind the others than to embarrass yourself – and your partner – by doing the wrong thing at the wrong time.

If the Loyal Toast offends your anti-monarchist principles, you should, at least, stand up. Any more obtrusive refusal shows an adolescent

disregard for the rules of hospitality. The Queen is unlikely to care if you remain glued to your seat waving a copy of the Little Red Book, but your host might.

After-dinner speeches follow the toast and should be approached with at least a willingness to be entertained; barracking, inappropriate laughing and bread roll throwing are very bad form. Even at regimental dinners, where a degree of rowdiness is expected, excessive high spirits are the preserve of the young and callow.

If the port decanter appears, not a drop must be drunk until after the Loyal Toast. Ancient tradition decrees that it must always be passed to the left; you should uphold this rule at all costs. If you happen to 'miss the boat', you can discreetly send your empty glass round the table after the bottle. On no account, however, should you send yourself after it. Much more stylish to pretend you never liked the stuff anyway.

WEEKENDS AWAY

You can look at romantic weekends in two ways: as a gesture of confidence in your relationship or as a test-pad for round-the-clock togetherness. Women will generally take the first view and are therefore thrilled when a man takes the initiative to arrange an escape *à deux*.

A surprise weekend away is even nicer, but don't leave the 'reveal' until the last moment, as your girlfriend will need to know roughly what to pack. Garlands will be heaped upon you if you choose a destination geared more to her pleasure than your own; the novice may not, for example, be thrilled by a weekend of potholing/fell walking.

City breaks are perfect for newish couples requiring talking points and cultural stimulus, though your girlfriend should never feel that she is less interesting than the programme.

Country/beach breaks work best when you're relaxed enough to enjoy quiet time together and require little entertainment other than each other.

If uninterrupted passion is your object (and why should it not be?), take her to Paris where it is practically de rigueur to kiss in the street.

A bit of advance groundwork on your trip will lend a devastating air of casual competence. Bookings should be double-checked/routes ready-memorised. You don't want to be so uptight about making sure everything is perfect that you have no time to enjoy your partner's company.

Some research about your destination is also advisable. Check out local restaurants and bars and choose accommodation in a safe and central location. Make sure you're up to speed on cultural highlights and have a few ideas about how you'll spend your days.

Setting out on a trip together creates a fellow-travellers' complicity which can be wildly sexy; the exception to this is car journeys where you expose your latent driving demons. Losing your temper with other drivers on the road – especially women drivers – is unlikely to impress your companion; flashing slower drivers and leaning on the horn is particularly excruciating. If, on the other hand, your partner is behind the wheel, it is impolite to grip the dashboard and cross yourself at every major junction.

Air travel is, on the whole, less fraught. It should be noted that, in the era of budget airlines, the 'mile-high' club has long since lost its glamour; roguish invitations to join are unlikely to impress. It's a good idea, when travelling to foreign cities with low-cost operators, to check that the airport is, in fact, within striking distance of the city; a surprise three-hour coach trip each way will make a heart-sinking hole in your weekend.

On arrival at your hotel, the booking should be checked – room type/rate, floor, view – to prevent unpleasant surprises. If things are not as expected, politely negotiate improvements – shouting at hotel staff will not improve the service during your stay.

As a final romantic flourish, pre-ordered champagne and flowers in the room cannot be bettered and may – who knows? – dispose your lady friend to kick-start the weekend with some very thoughtful gestures of her own.

VILLA BREAKS

Sharing a villa with friends is the ultimate test of couple-compatibility. It is almost inevitable that one of you will be more at home with the group than the other, and the incomer is under strain of prolonged scrutiny. If time *à deux* is not set aside for necessary venting, one of you will go mad.

In a self-catered villa, division of labour is key. A rota for chores/cooking and a kitty for any household expenses may be a rather formal way of starting a holiday, but it is infinitely better than some members of the party feeling martyred while others wonder what all the black looks are about.

'Bagging' the biggest and best room is rude. It's customary for the person who arranged the holiday/accommodation to have first dibs. Otherwise, unless there are clear reasons why some rooms are better suited to certain people (couples/singles etc.), it's fairer to draw lots.

Your girlfriend will not appreciate it if you bond too enthusiastically with the other men in the party and stay up every night until the small hours watching sport and playing drinking games.

While a quarrelling couple can spoil a villa holiday for everyone, an overly amorous couple is almost worse. A romantic siesta after lunch is perfectly acceptable. If you're still at the stage of retiring after breakfast, you're probably better off in a hotel.

SKIING

It is highly probable that one half of a couple will be better at skiing than the other, but it's not a competition. If your companion is the expert, accept this with good grace. Raise your game, by all means, but don't attempt manoeuvres beyond your capabilities for the sake of keeping face as an injury will spoil the fun for both of you.

If you are the more experienced skier, resist the call of the black run (or at least leave it for later). This is not the time for showing off. Pick the most appropriate route for your partner and lead her down the mountain. If it looks too obviously patronising to ski at her pace, plot a course of staging posts (clearly visible from above) where you can wait for her to catch you up while ostensibly admiring the Alpine scenery.

Teaching a novice to ski is much like dealing with a learner driver; calm encouragement and superhuman reserves of patience will move things along much faster than barked instructions and vein-throbbing irritation. A degree of humour can help enormously, but take care to laugh only when she does.

On chairlifts, it is chivalrous to secure adjoining seats and to take responsibility for raising and lowering the safety bar. On button lifts – the kind where one person goes at a time – you should always let the lady go first. That way you can keep an eye on her ascent and quickly leap to her rescue if she runs into difficulties.

Unless your companion is struggling (or plain exhausted) it is not necessary to carry her skis for her; the attraction of playing the hero must be weighed against the increased likelihood of your stumbling under the weight of two lots of equipment.

Piste etiquette should be observed at all times. The person ahead has right of way. If you are visibly annoying other skiers by zooming past them too fast/too close, your girlfriend will be more embarrassed than impressed.

Queuing for food in ski-cafés is not very entertaining. It will be appreciated as an act of true chivalry if you fetch the lunch while your girlfriend sits down at a table and enjoys the mountain air.

Après-ski, too, is frequently less chic than it sounds. If you are both equally keen on getting drenched with sweat/beer in a hot, crowded bar, plunge right in. Be sensitive to what your girlfriend may want/not want to do after a long day on the slopes; a big night out may not be what she has in mind. A sundowner on the slopes before heading back to the chalet for shower, dinner and drinks in front of the log fire (nothing like a fire to bring out the inner caveman) is a more romantically interesting option.

YACHTING

Maybe it's the tanned feet in deckshoes, maybe it's the sheer ruinous expense of it all, but there's nothing like a yacht to boost a man's attractions. An invitation to sail into the sunset is usually a sure-fire winner. Even if the reality of narrow bunks and chemical loos comes as a bit of a let down, it's something every girl wants to try at least once.

If you're the captain of the boat, you make the rules. It's not being arrogant, it's expected. It may take some getting used to on the part of your girlfriend, however, if you start bossing her about the boat, so try to go easy on your newest deck-hand.

If you're a guest on the boat, you must follow procedure to the letter. It's dangerous not to. You will also find that yachtsmen take their jargon terribly seriously – 'sheet' for rope, 'head' for loo etc. – and expect you to join in. A moment's self-consciousness as you request 'permission to board' (you really do have to say that) is a very small price to pay for the chance to experience life as a bona fide babe-magnet.

Unless the yacht is fully crewed, you and your girlfriend will be expected to muck in and take direction from the captain. Canoodling on deck while there's a mainbrace to be

spliced will go down badly. Canoodling below deck, for that matter, requires considerate restraint as cabin walls are paper thin.

Water supplies are likely to be limited, so long, luxurious showers are out and there may be strict rules concerning use of the lavatory/'head'. Booze, too, may be rationed or at least less plentiful than usual; hangovers and sea-swells are a killer combination.

Even when there is a full complement of deckhands and cooks, help clearing up is always appreciated. It is also courteous when aboard ship to stow your possessions tidily

and keep them stowed away except when they're in use.

If you're putting in to port at night, buying dinner at a restaurant is an appropriate gesture to your hosts. At the end of the evening, you should find your berth quietly and decorously. Sounds carry easily over water.

On leaving, tip all the crew via the captain, who will advise you on a suitable gratuity depending on the length of your stay and the level of service you enjoyed. A written thank you to the host should follow promptly – sailors are sticklers for correct drill.

SPORTING EVENTS

POLO

The 'sport of kings' has special cachet for girls (given the high concentration of rich men in tight trousers the reason for this cachet is not, perhaps, so elusive). You don't have to be an expert for the glamour to rub off, but you should know what's going on out there. It's no more complicated than any other game involving balls and goals: you just have to remember that the teams are called 'quartets' and it's 'ponies', never 'horses'. A game is divided into 'chukkas' and each chukka lasts seven minutes. Polo players, like golfers, are given handicaps ranging from minus two (least whizzy) to 10 (probably Argentinian). There are two mounted umpires in striped shirts.

Polo is played from April to September, making it the perfect excuse for a picnic. Grandstand seats are available but it's worth buying/talking your way into the members' enclosure, where the dress code is at the smarter end of casual for men and prime tea-dress territory for women. If your partner fancies a spot of divot-stomping (at half-time, grass kicked up by the ponies is traditionally trodden back in by gigglesome girls), she should choose her footwear accordingly.

ROYAL ASCOT

If you wish to impress your consort with tickets to the Royal Enclosure, you need to start networking. Entry is restricted to those who have previously attended the Royal Enclosure or who have been nominated by an entry badge holder with at least four seasons under their belt. Tickets to Ladies' Day sell out almost as soon as they are released.

Dress code in the Royal Enclosure is famously strict; ladies must wear a formal day dress (nothing too skimpy) and a hat that covers the crown of the head. Men are required to wear black or grey morning dress and a top hat. Overseas visitors may wear their formal national dress.

In the Grandstand men should wear a suit or jacket and tie. Ladies may wear trousers, and hats are optional, though popular. For the Silver Ring and Heath Enclosure the code is rather more relaxed but, since your girlfriend will probably appreciate the chance to dress up to the nines, it seems a shame not to enter into the spirit of the occasion. Jeans, trainers and t-shirts with amusing slogans are not an option.

HENLEY REGATTA

For the Stewards' Enclosure, men must wear a lounge suit or blazer with flannels and a tie. If you are, or have been, a member of a rowing club at school or university, by all means sport your boating blazer (provided you can still get into it – straining seams and popping buttons detract from raffish charm). Otherwise a plain navy blazer is fine. For the towpath and Regatta Enclosure, both of which are open to the public, there is no formal dress code, but a nod to the spirit of the occasion is generally appreciated by your female companions.

TENNIS

Wimbledon and Queen's are stylish, summery venues for a date. Unless you are both die-hard tennis demons, it is not necessary – and hard on the neck – to watch every match, so don't go overboard about getting your money's worth. Pick the matches you really want to see and spend the rest of the time soaking up the atmosphere. Sink a Pimm's or two, feed your girl the world's most expensive strawberries and it'll be 'Love All' before the rain comes.

RUGBY/CRICKET/FOOTBALL

If your partner is not in the habit of attending these events, it is probable that she is only going to humour you. Return the compliment by making the occasion as entertaining as possible. Outlining the rules may help in this regard, as may relevant facts about the players and the team, but be alert to signals such as eye glazing/shoulder slumping/outright sobbing from your lady friend.

It is considerate too, to clue her in on team colours – she won't understand if you bundle her into a raincoat just because she's wearing a fashionable approximation of the 'enemy's' strip. She may well underestimate just how cold and hard on the feet these events can be, so make sure she has suitable footwear and extra layers of clothing.

If your team loses, she may hazard the dangerous opinion that it's not the end of the world. She doesn't really mean it, it's her hormones that stop her being as viscerally affected ('gutted' in boy-speak) as you. Just try not to cry until you get home.

TIPS TO REMEMBER

Don't get into a state about tipping. There's an accepted tariff for gratuities and it should be costed in to the date.

In restaurants with no service charge, the general rule is 10–15 per cent in the UK. Withholding service charges should only be considered in the case of extreme negligence or rudeness. If you feel that the food was below par, tip the waiting staff anyway (it's not their fault). Address your complaints to the manager, who may adjust the bill accordingly.

In black cabs and mini cabs, the going rate for tips is 10 per cent.

Hotel bellboys expect one unit of currency – e.g. one pound/dollar/euro – per case, given to them as they leave the room. Doormen should also be tipped one unit for calling a cab and a larger sum on leaving the hotel at the end of your visit.

Room service delivery comes in at around two units for a meal and one unit for drinks.

Leave a banknote for housekeeping (five units for short stays, a bit more for longer) in your hotel room, not with reception, at the end of your stay. This will ensure that it reaches the right person.

It's always a good idea, on arrival in a foreign country, to furnish yourself with a number of small denomination bank notes. There is nothing more embarrassing than flashing a huge wad of money at local staff while miming that you have nothing small enough to give them.

GOING PUBLIC

Y ou never thought it would happen to you, but gradually 'we' is replacing 'I' in your thoughts and conversation. Declaring yourself part of a couple is a major step and needs careful management if claustrophobia – or outright panic – is to be avoided.

Presenting a united front need not mean losing your identity. It certainly shouldn't mean losing old friends. A degree of autonomy is normal and necessary in new relationships.

With the right combination of togetherness and trust, life *à deux* can be so much more than the sum of the parts.

FACING THE WORLD

Being a couple does not mean being joined at the hip. It does, however, mean presenting a united front to the world. You may not share our opinions on everything from politics to food preferences (indeed, it would be slightly bizarre if you did), but we need to know that, fundamentally, you're 'on our side'.

It is very easy, particularly in the first flush of coupledom, to confuse candour with indiscretion. Sharing secrets is a thrilling part of the bonding process, but your new and enhanced knowledge of your girlfriend's inner self should never be displayed as a badge of 'togetherness'.

Confidentiality between couples is crucial. And it's a fair bet that more is confidential than you might presume. Just because she was laughing when she told you about the

time she split her gym knickers at school doesn't mean she'll laugh when you regale your mates with the same story.

Similarly, divulging too much information about her friends, family or workmates ('ah so you're the one with the eating disorder/unfortunate fetish for stationery reps') should be avoided – these are private revelations and should be kept in the vault.

Equally bad form is the 'show tiff' – the larky spat intended to show how 'relaxed' you are with your partner. This makes for a poor spectator sport and inevitably leads to real recrimination behind closed doors. If you are genuinely upset by something your girlfriend says or does in the company of others, you should pretend, if possible, not to notice. Resolve the matter later on when you're in

private if it's still bothering you. A useful mantra in this dangerous situation is 'don't start'. The essential skill, which must be practised, is in saying it yourself before your girlfriend says it out loud.

At all events, avoid the hands raised in the air gesture ('What? What have I done?') beloved of continental footballers in the aftermath of a foul. Your friends are not referees.

In general debate, try to avoid consistently taking another's part against us (particularly another woman's part). If we feel you are 'ganging up' with friends against us, we will question your motives and your commitment to the relationship.

Generalised gallantry to females in the party is fine – we like you to be social – but this should not tip over into extended flirting with our friends. We will notice, they will notice and you will be forever branded an evil rat by the sisterhood.

Over time, a couple develops its own code of signals for use in tricky social situations. Some rules of couple conduct are, however, internationally recognised (at least by all women).

If we join your conversation with another woman, we are, in the nicest possible way, claiming you as our own. We therefore expect to be promptly introduced with due honour. If you don't, we will immediately become a little bit suspicious.

If, *par contre*, we wave you over from the other side of the room and make a big deal of introducing you as our boyfriend, we are probably crying out to be rescued. If we remark on the lateness of the hour, it means we want to go home (with you). 'Gosh, I'm tired' is girl-speak for 'Get me out of here NOW'. If our every subtle hint is ignored and we are forced to leave on our own, be aware that our casual sounding 'bye then' is likely to be definitive.

GOING SOLO

It's healthy for couples to go their separate ways on occasion. The modern woman is wary of men who have no interests or social life of their own. At the same time, we do not wish to play the widow to your many sporting, social and professional engagements. Most importantly, we never want to feel like the 'default' entertainment.

Synchronising diaries, except for big events and holidays, is unnecessarily formal and claustrophobic at the start of a relationship, but it is polite to keep your girlfriend in the loop about your planned activities.

Be specific and generous with detail, as a casual approach ('just hanging out with the lads' or 'seeing someone for a drink') may be interpreted as avoidance. Conversely, while it is good form to show an interest in your partner's 'other life', your concern should not tip over into possessiveness.

Calling/texting her when you know she's on a big night out, or checking up to see what time she gets home only makes you look insecure. A relaxed 'catch up' call in the

morning, however, lets her know that she's in your thoughts (and she will be particularly flattered if you have remembered what it was she was doing).

Above all, you must never lie or appear cagey about where you're going or who you are seeing; indeed the only thing worse than this is lying about where and with whom you have been. Either infraction will queer the pitch for future solo excursions.

If you're planning a holiday or weekend away without your increasingly significant other, adequate notice must be given (in the case of a week or two's summer holiday, this means months – not days – as your partner will be making plans of her own). Nor will she be best pleased if she finds you packing your lucky pants for that conference you have been dreading but 'just can't get out of'.

It's a good idea to mix your freelance activities with thoughtfully planned entertainments *à deux*. It will also be reassuring if some of your companions are known to your girlfriend. If they're known to be in stable relationships of their own, so much the better.

Should you fall among unsuitable company and find yourself hauled into a strip joint/lap-dancing club, own up immediately – it is not something we want to find out from a third party, but spare us the details. Don't slag off the paid entertainment (you're the one, after all, who was paying for it) but neither should you dwell on their professional expertise. You probably found it all terribly boring but, if a single memory rises from the mists of tedium, let it be that none of the women were a patch on us.

FRIENDSHIPS

The merging of old friendships with a new relationship requires tact and skill. You may be utterly incurious about the social network of your new girlfriend. She, however, will take a forensic interest in yours.

It is a good idea to introduce friends as gradually and informally as possible. A dinner party where you are the only person your girlfriend knows will leave her feeling exposed and convinced that the company is holding up scorecards the minute she leaves the room. Nor should you invite her along to an event where your friends are expecting to see you alone.

Meeting up with one or two easygoing friends for a movie and dinner is perfect as there will be a fresh topic for conversation where everyone is on an equal footing. By all means clue her in on your friends' backgrounds and

how you know them, but don't brief her as if she's going to a summit meeting.

On an occasion when your partner is with people she either doesn't know or knows only slightly, it's up to you to keep the conversation general and inclusive. Watch out for her and check she's coping – always wade in if she's stuck with a bore. 'In-jokes' are never ever made funnier by explanation. Other people's work problems run a close second to other people's night-time dreams for sheer, head-banging tedium.

An exception to the 'keep it general' rule can, however, be made for discussion of affairs of the heart – this is an area where most women feel comfortable and authoritative.

Do not be surprised/offended if your partner jumps to instant and far-reaching conclusions

about the people she has just met; the female mind works considerably faster than the male in this regard and it doesn't mean she won't change her mind about somebody on deeper acquaintance.

If, on the other hand, she conceives a lasting dislike for an individual or for a particular group of your friends, the situation will require close analysis and crisis management. A simple personality clash has an equally simple solution – you continue to see these friends on your own.

If the real problem is that your consort doesn't like the way you behave when you are with these friends, and if, to put it baldly, she thinks they are 'a bad influence', then you might find it politic to modify your response to the group dynamic when she is around.

Nothing good can come of telling your mates that your partner doesn't like them. And vice versa. Particularly vice versa. Either way, it just makes it more awkward. If, despite your best efforts, it comes to a full-blown mates *v* soulmate stand-off, your first loyalty is to the person you want to spend most time with in the future.

Deep down, women are attracted – possibly more than men – to the idea of close male friendship. You should be able to discuss your relationship with a trusted friend (trusted, that is, by both you and your girlfriend) but we'd prefer it if you discussed it with us first.

When it comes to sex, women of the world know that men talk, and so long as you keep it unspecific and complimentary (and only discuss it when we're not present) we're not really in a position to mind since we will be keeping up a lively commentary with our own close friends.

And of course, we can always keep it running longer than you.

VISITING THE FAMILY

If you've been asked to meet the family, things are getting serious. If you feel unready for this important step, it's kinder to decline the invitation. Nervous attempts to 'downplay' the relationship in front of your girlfriend's family will appear more caddish than casual.

On introduction, a firm handshake and 'how do you do' goes down better with parents than a breezy 'hi'. First name terms should be adopted by invitation only. It is no bad idea to keep up the 'Mr and Mrs Jones' routine until you are cordially begged to stop, as this will give the encouraging impression of 'a nicely brought-up boy'. For similar reasons, chewing gum, swearing, sniffing, chair-tipping and other boyhood behaviour your own parents warned you against should be avoided.

Ask for a full rundown on eccentricities and deeply held opinions in advance of your introduction and, unless you're sure of shared views, avoid the traditional touchpapers of politics and religion. Talking about your job shows commendable drive, but should never tip over into boasting or competitiveness with other males.

If stuck for conversation, talk – in the most affectionate terms – about your girlfriend. If a wily family member throws you a googly, inviting you to join in family banter about your beloved's terrible time-keeping/organisational skills, keep your wits about you: the right response is to pronounce her the pinnacle of female perfection. Anything less and your intentions and sincerity may be questioned.

If you have been invited to her family home, always take a present. Flowers or chocolates are a safe option and can be better than wine as there is less risk of appearing flash, stingy or tasteless. Offer – but do not insist on – help with cooking and clearing up. Some hosts don't like strangers venturing 'behind the scenes'. On subsequent visits, when you are more familiar and have been 'accepted' into the fold, you should get on and help without comment.

At a restaurant, on her family's invitation, be suitably grateful and delighted by all the arrangements but do not offer to pay or leave a tip as this may be construed as an attempt to 'take over' from the host.

FAMILY
MANNERS

Good manners of the door-holding kind go a long way with mothers, but chivalry should not slide into intergenerational flirting, especially in the presence of fathers who are apt to characterise overt charm as 'oily'.

Too much physical affection bestowed on your girlfriend will be filed under 'pawing'. In all other respects, genuine attentiveness to your partner cannot be overdone, particularly under the sharp gaze of the fond mama who will be quick to notice any dereliction of affectionate duty.

Sisters are famously tricky. Your aim, here, is to engage on an impeccably asexual level; if there are any nephews and nieces around, extravagant praise of their many fine qualities will not go amiss, otherwise stick to current affairs. Brothers, on the whole, respond to commonplace blokey topics such as sport and work.

In the event that it all goes horribly wrong and you flirt with her father and fight with her mother, do not panic. Going horribly wrong is what family gatherings do best.

When debriefing with your girlfriend, always remember the golden rule: she may criticise her family, you may not. As far as you're concerned, the entire crew of snobs, slobs, tarts and knucklegrazers are 'marvellous characters' and you can't wait to meet them all again. Because they won't be going away. And a long truce is easier than a long fight.

OTHER WOMEN

Behind every good man is a collection of good women. But what if they don't get on? Your relationship to other women in your social, professional and family network is crucial to your relationship with your girlfriend. Each has their own claim on your affections and you need them all on side.

Treating the women in your life with equal respect, while at the same time making your partner feel special, requires a plate-spinner's vigilance and vast reserves of tact.

Consider the chances of one man against an outraged female phalanx, and you'll see it's a skill worth perfecting.

SISTERS

Your sister is your earliest source of insight into the feminine psyche. She is also the one who knows where the bodies are buried. As such, she requires careful handling. When your girlfriend is introduced to your sister, it is important that neither should feel that too much is riding on the meeting. Your sister needs to know that she is not being displaced as a comrade in arms. Your girlfriend should never be made to feel that your sister has any 'right of veto' on your relationship.

Falling immediately into the rut of childhood jokes and excessive 'do you remembers?' is inconsiderate. Your partner may learn to love your family routines but cannot be expected, straight off the bat, to appreciate the hilarity of the time Aunt Mary got stuck on the ski-lift. Conversely, your sister may feel obscurely cross at being 'excluded' from your new life as part of a couple ('well, you never used to like sushi!'). It is your job, at such times, to lead the conversation back to neutral ground.

It may well be that the single thing your sister and your girlfriend have in common is *you*, which, however appealing as a subject, is soon exhausted. Don't be hurt if the two of them don't love each other on sight. They may never be best friends and it is pointless to force an affinity where none exists. If they go toe-to-toe, then chivalry demands that you defend your partner's corner. If the situation is intractable, you may be better off seeing your sister alone until the bad feeling blows over.

In the happy event that your sibling and your sweetheart get on like a house on fire, allow them space to cement the friendship. Accept that it's part of the feminine bonding process to gang up on men. Make the most of their friendship; it can only be helpful to have a female perspective on what your consort really likes in the way of birthday presents, surprise outings or underwear.

Take heart, too, from the encouraging fact that if your partner likes your family, she will be more inclined to see you as a long term option. The positives of this useful alliance overwhelmingly outweigh the fact that every time you see them laugh together, you'll think they're laughing at you. And you'll probably be right.

MOTHERS

Freud had a point. All men are mummy's boys *au fond*. Success with women depends largely on how you manage this crucial relationship. The way a man treats his mother sends clear signals to a potential mate about his attitude to women in general.

Accept the fact that, to your mother, you will always be a child (you can rail against it, but it won't make a blind bit of difference). Your partner, on the other hand, has signed up for a man. It is a conundrum only you can solve.

The filial image you want to project is one of affectionate independence. It will not enhance your profile as an alpha male if your mum still washes your clothes and cuts your hair. Nor is it attractive in a man to be constantly seeking maternal approval (particularly in the matter of who you choose to go out with and how you conduct your life as a couple).

Respect, however, or at the least kindness, is due to mothers. Even if you are not close, it is your adult responsibility to keep in touch and look out for her comfort. If you are close, be careful not to revert to truculent adolescence the minute you return to the maternal fold. Your teenage girlfriends may have found it rather thrilling and impressively rebellious when you crashed upstairs to listen to loud records and refused to come down for tea. Your grown-up partner, left to make polite conversation, almost certainly will not.

In the event of a clash between your mother and your love interest, it is best to avoid the appearance of 'siding' with either party. Try to discuss the problem, in private, with each of them. 'Having it all out in the open' rarely helps, as any momentary satisfaction your mother or girlfriend may feel in publicly trumping the other will be cancelled out by many long, painful years of pretending it never happened. Keep in mind that while you have a lifetime's love banked against disagreements with your mother, your partner has no such advantage.

Above all, if you wish to maintain any kind of erotic life, you should avoid treating your lover like your mother. Oedipus, you will recall, confused the two most important women in his life – and all he ended up with was a complex.

FEMALE BOSSES

Manners towards a female boss are important as this is a relationship which quickly exposes male insecurities and chauvinism. Your partner may not have the opportunity to observe you in the workplace, but the way you talk about your boss is revealing about your attitudes to women and their place in society.

It is imperative, for the good of your career and your relationship, that you show precisely the degree of respect and professionalism towards a female superior that you would to a male. Ascribing questionable executive decisions to the effects of PMT/sexual frustration/the menopause won't secure your advancement in either boardroom or bedroom.

Successful women are frighteningly alert to any hint of chippiness from male juniors. In fact, the only thing worse than a chippy junior is a junior who thinks he can condescend to, or seduce, his boss. Sex – or indeed any kind of sexual allusion – is totally inappropriate as a means of resolving office tensions. Even flirting with a superior is out of the question (unless you actively wish to be branded 'office totty'). During office hours some modification of your customary gallantry may be necessary (or at least prudent).

Standing up when your female boss enters the room or flinging yourself into her path to open doors is unnecessary and possibly inadvisable as any behaviour which draws attention to gender differences may be frowned upon.

Should you find yourself in a cultural context where men and women do not generally have equal roles (i.e. meetings with foreign clients or business trips abroad), it is important that you continue to show due deference to your female superior. Don't attempt to take charge or assume the role of 'protector' unless she clearly requests that you do so.

On occasions where you meet your boss in a purely social context, feel free to be your usual chivalrous self; the alteration in your manner will serve only to point out your careful observation of office protocol and can do you no harm at all. No one ever said chivalry was for the benefit of just one sex.

COLLEAGUES

The evolved male will refer to his female colleagues as 'women', not 'ladies' and never 'girls'. In an office where there are more men than women, you should go out of your way to promote an inclusive atmosphere; the important discussion of Chelsea v Arsenal/ Porsche v Ferrari/suspenders v hold-ups is better saved for the pub.

In all but the most strait-laced environments, a little light flirting *among equals* will not go amiss, but care must be taken that special attentions to junior colleagues are not seen as an abuse of your position. You may think it the most natural thing to boost a young co-worker with a fatherly pat or encouraging squeeze; she may see it differently and your partner, should she hear of it, is likely to have her own strong views on the matter.

Similarly, the 'office wife' syndrome needs to be carefully managed. It is not uncommon to build a particularly close and confidential relationship with a female colleague, but the boundaries of this supportive friendship must be clearly delineated. Your girlfriend will not appreciate it if your evenings alone together are consistently interrupted by long, intense phone calls with another woman, however impeccably professional the context.

While you have every right to keep your home and work life separate, your partner should be known – at least in concept – to your workmates. If she accompanies you to a work function and your colleagues are totally amazed to find that you're in a proper and serious relationship, she is well within her own rights to revise the terms of your contract.

EXES

When it comes to ex girlfriends, the current incumbent's first thought will invariably be 'who dumped whom, and why?'. Again, honesty is the best policy, especially if your ex is still part of your life.

The perfect time for the crucial first meeting between your ex and your girlfriend is when the latter is looking her absolute best. Ideally, the two of you'll be on your way to a fabulous party when you bump into your ex, who will be out jogging in her foulest tracksuit. Failing this, a more relaxed, group situation is less pressurised than a three-way summit and, if the two women don't get on, at least they don't have to spend the whole time spitting pleasantries at each other.

When your girlfriend is present, steer clear of memory lane. You and your ex will naturally have news to exchange, but the emphasis should be on your lives now. If your ex is also in a new relationship, a few brief references to what 'we' are doing for 'our' holiday etc. will be quietly appreciated by your partner. If your ex is currently single, however, this starts to look like (and probably is) point scoring.

No matter how amicable the split, or how long ago it happened, it really is less than reassuring to your girlfriend if you spend a lot of time in one-to-one situations with your ex; a 'catch-up' drink after work is fine. Dinner starts to look like a date.

If the split was bitter, you should be very obviously over it by now. The last thing your girlfriend wants to hear is you wondering how it all went wrong, or explaining how hurt you were, or how just hearing your ex's voice brings you out in a rash... These are not the marks of a man who has moved on.

It is never a good plan to have photographs of your ex displayed at home, but stashing them in obvious hiding places (under sofa cushions, in bedside drawers etc.) is almost worse. The same goes for obviously sexy gifts from another era.

Most women will accept that most men have had some kind of romantic past; it's how you process that past that counts. 'Older but wiser' is usually a good look. Work it to your advantage.

FEMALE FRIENDS

The question almost certainly burning in your girlfriend's brain when introduced to 'a close friend who happens to be a girl' is 'have you slept with her?'. Any fibbing, in this ticklish situation, is nearly always a disaster.

Whether you have or haven't done the deed, it should be very clear, from your demeanour, that this, right now, is the farthest thing from your mind. Even if your relationship with 'the friend who's a girl' is based entirely on suppressed sexual tension, and particularly if she's 'the one who got away', your behaviour towards her in the presence of your anointed 'other half' should never stray beyond the comradely.

It should not become apparent, in the course of the introduction, that your friend is *au fait* with every step of your new relationship. If

you have been in the habit of sharing your experiences in this way with her, it is a habit which now needs to stop. Unless your female friend is unusually clueless about the nature of human relations, she will understand the necessity for this new distance between you and withdraw gracefully. If she cuts up rough, it is up to you to define the boundaries.

In the event that a friend doesn't get on with your new partner and makes no attempt to hide it, there's no good in preparing a lengthy defence of your old mate's many excellent qualities or explaining that she has been unlucky in love. Your girlfriend won't want to hear it and, in all fairness, she shouldn't have to.

If things are being made difficult for her within your wider social circle, it may help if you ask another, less troubled, female friend to look out for your girlfriend and make her feel part of things and, possibly, broker a better understanding with her antagonist. It is crucial that your partner and close friends find a way to get on or your social life, as a couple, will become increasingly tricky as the relationship progresses.

Understand that even the most unconflicted and impeccably platonic friendships will undergo a slight realignment once you're part of a couple. The rules change; certain codes of behaviour that were once perfectly fine suddenly become unacceptable.

The fact that you don't, never have and never will fancy a certain girl does not make it all right, for example, to share a bed/hotel room/tent with her, no matter how exceptional the circumstances. It doesn't matter that you were snowed in, ran out of petrol or that a dog ate her sleeping bag – your girlfriend will not understand. Defensiveness, on your part, will make a bad situation worse.

If in doubt as to the propriety of a situation, try the 'how would I feel in her place?' trick. Don't cheat and make yourself feel better by factoring in her least attractive friend. The chances are, no matter who he is, you wouldn't like it.

If, on the other hand, you feel your partner is being unduly possessive (and yes, there is such a thing as due possessiveness) there is no harm in gently pointing out that you are uncomfortable with her behaviour. Just don't expect more than is humanly possible.

THE GIRLFRIEND'S BEST FRIEND

The GBF can make or break your relationship. Suspicion and criticism are often her default position, so you're going to have to work hard at getting her on-side.

First, you should concede unreservedly that she knows your girlfriend better than you do. You will get nowhere with the GBF until this important point is settled. If she doesn't like you, redouble your efforts to please, but make sure your charm offensive is not confused with attempted seduction as this will play very badly with both GBF and girlfriend. Even if you have good reason to suspect the GBF of real malevolence, bite your lip as a feud will only make your girlfriend miserable and an ultimatum ('it's her or me!') can only ever sound hysterical.

Going out in a foursome with the GBF's other half is one way of spreading the emotional overload. Otherwise keep an impeccably friendly distance and let your girlfriend see the meddling harridan on her own.

Should you gain her good opinion, however, the GBF is a sound ally. She is the one your girlfriend is going to moan to when things are less than perfect in your relationship and her positive intervention is invaluable.

However well you get on, remember whose best friend she is. It is a mistake for you to moan about any aspect, however trifling, of your love life to the GBF – not least because it'll go straight back to your girlfriend before you've even had time to add the bit about how much you adore her anyway.

There will inevitably be occasions when you are obliged to witness the GBF's romantic crises. While you should give every impression of support, your role, here, is essentially non-speaking. Expressions of blokeish solidarity ('look at it his way,' 'the chap has a point') are unwanted and irrelevant. Far better to pour two large glasses of wine and leave before it is noticed that if all men are emotional cripples you must be one too.

MOVING IN TOGETHER

Ying You can't live without her. But living with her takes some getting used to. How were you to know, until you merged the wardrobe, that she arranges her clothes by colour? And what is this business of candles round the bath? Is it some kind of cult or simple fear of electrocution?

Of course it's lovely to entertain your friends in a proper home. And it's kind of cute the way your toothbrushes sit side by side on the bathroom shelf.

So what if the bedroom looks like Barbie's boudoir and there are bras drying on the bike rack. She's just so nice to come home to...

ADAPTING TO COHABITATION

Certain assumptions about how your partner likes to live may require some fine-tuning now that you're living together. She may not, for example, have commented on the sock recycling system favoured in your bachelor flat (kick the dirty socks to the corner of the room, and when they've worked their way back to the middle they're ready to wear); this does not mean that she intends to sleep in a fug of feet from now on. Similarly, the 'bare essentials' beauty regime she followed while staying over at your place may not have prepared you for the amount of bathroom time required for daily maintenance.

If you're moving into a new place together, it's relatively easy to establish an agreed modus operandi. If one of you is moving into the other's home, a degree of tongue-biting is inevitable. Initially, at least, a certain amount of independence built into your living arrangements will help – you don't want to feel like you're living in one another's pockets.

Privacy, particularly in relation to mail/emails and phone calls, should be respected. Over time, personal domains will evolve within the home, but a territorial land-grab on moving-in day ('the kitchen is my space – you can have the bedroom') is unlikely to be helpful.

If you are moving into your girlfriend's home and you don't like the décor, there's not much you can do except remodel by attrition – a picture here, an armchair there – until you are more comfortable with your surroundings. If you're starting with a clean slate and find yourselves head-to-head on design matters, you need to examine your motives. Are you both genuinely passionate about the project? Do you care that much, or are you just asserting rights because you can? A compromise is rarely the happiest design solution, so if one of you feels you can 'give a little', it's well worth doing.

Certain aspects of your lifestyle will necessarily change now that you're living together. It isn't fair, for example, to pile back home from the pub with a bunch of mates bearing six-packs without clearing it first with your girlfriend. Indeed the only thing worse than this is piling back for an impromptu party and then complaining about catering arrangements ('how come there's no bread for bacon sandwiches?').

It goes without saying that modern women expect domestic chores to be equally shared – in principle, at any rate. If your girlfriend assumes more than her share of shopping, cooking etc., remember it's a favour and thank her. Manners – small, daily observances which show consideration – are arguably more important at this stage of the relationship than at any other. Living together should never be the cue for taking one another for granted.

BEHAVIOURAL ADJUSTMENT

Now that you're sharing a home, certain bachelor habits will bear revision, including:

Hogging the remote; nowhere is it written that sport takes precedence over every other programme on the television. We are likely to make an exception for big, one-off sporting events, but a game of football between recently emerged nation states playing each other in some godforsaken spot that only satellite will reach does not constitute a big match. Nor do computer console games make riveting spectator sport. Buying us a telly to watch in the kitchen is not the answer.

Bi-annual laundry blitzes; laundry should be done as it occurs, not when you have nothing but pyjamas left to wear. Sports kit/team shirts etc. should be washed immediately after use. Bed sheets, tea towels and bath towels need to be washed at least as regularly as clothes. We will take it very badly if you gather up your own clothes for washing and leave the household linen to fester.

Surface sweeps; just because something is reasonably tidy, it doesn't mean it's clean. Bathroom and kitchen cleanliness is non-negotiable. Loos need to be scrubbed before

they look dirty. The same goes for food preparation areas. When sharing a bathroom it is especially important to rinse baths/basins after use. Even if we love every hair on your head, we will love them considerably less when we're picking them from the plug-hole, and the same goes for the attractive foam-and-stubble sediment left after shaving.

Pre-soak procrastinations; jamming dirty dishes into the sink and leaving them there is not any kind of useful preamble to washing up. Filling up the sink with water only makes it worse as grease is transferred from dinner plates to glasses etc. and the whole operation takes twice as long when you (or we, if you leave it so long that we 'break') finally get round to doing it.

Storage snatching; filling up more than half the wardrobe/drawer space with your clothes (particularly if a significant proportion of these will clearly never be worn but are being kept in case they come back into fashion) is irritating. Clothes are our area of speciality and we will expect the lion's share of available storage. Piles on the floor, however orderly, are not a workable solution.

IN THE KITCHEN

Any number of celebrity chefs attest to the super-competence of men in the kitchen. The downside of this is that you can no longer get away with boyish bewilderment when faced with a garlic press or unpeeled prawn. If cooking is not a pleasure for you, you should not assume (although it may be true) that it's less of a pain for your partner.

The well-stocked kitchen is a shared chore. We shouldn't have to write an exhaustive list for you every time you do the supermarket run. Nor does it contribute to any sense of togetherness if we have to talk you through each and every purchase on your mobile. You should know when essentials are running low and replenish supplies of pasta, rice, salad, fruit etc. Other stock cupboard stalwarts include olive oil, balsamic vinegar, eggs, parmesan, capers and dried chillies; the idea being the ability to conjure a simple meal from nothing at a moment's notice.

Simple meals, we recognise, are not what men enjoy cooking. A meal is not a meal, for a certain type of competitive male, unless it involves barricading yourself in the kitchen for

three hours with ruinously exotic ingredients and more precision-engineered equipment than NASA. It is particularly irksome when men insist on doing things 'from scratch', such as festooning the kitchen with hand-made pasta when the cupboards are bulging with packets of the dried stuff.

Women do not, on the whole, consider it a matter of pride to eat the hottest curry or the biggest, bloodiest steak and we just don't get it when men treat the table like a field of honour. We may even be grateful for smaller portions and certainly don't mean it as an insult if we cannot clear our hub-cap sized plate. It's also worth remembering that things take longer to cook in real kitchens than they do on telly. You may have the temperamental, pan-rattling gestures off to a T, but food doesn't cook any quicker if you shout at it.

Of course it's lovely when the smoke clears, your girlfriend is allowed back into the kitchen and the two of you sit down to a gourmet experience. Preparing simpler meals, together, is a quieter pleasure, but one that warms the heart of the home.

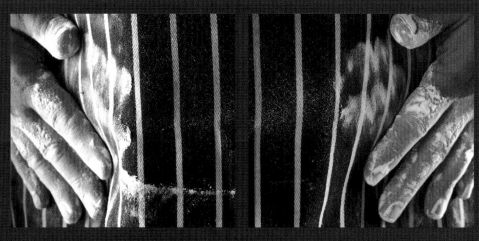

BEING A HOST

One of the joys of setting up home together is being able to entertain guests in your own style. It's worth remembering, though, that successful entertaining isn't just about mixing the perfect Martini. Your partner will be less than entranced if she is left to do the boring bits – shopping/cooking/clearing up while you dispense drinks and *bons mots*.

If you have invited guests over (particularly if you have invited your family), it is primarily up to you to look after them. It may be that your girlfriend is happy to do the feeding and watering while you do 'front of house' (or vice versa), but she should never be left to run the whole show on her own.

If your mother is in the party, your girlfriend will be particularly keen to impress; make sure you publicly praise her culinary skills and show that you are 'on her side'. On no account should Mum be invited – or even allowed – to take over the kitchen (you may need to step in here if it happens).

Nor is it acceptable, in your new co-habiting role, to barricade yourself in the the other room to take 'urgent' calls, invent emergency appointments in the pub or otherwise slide offside the minute your partner's friends and family hove into view. It's a two-person team now you're living together; muck in or expect trouble when everyone else has gone home.

If you are having people to stay, it is your responsibility, as a solicitous host, to wait on them for the first day, making sure they are not thirsty, cold or bored. Thereafter it may be more relaxing for everyone if you let them know they are welcome to make themselves at home.

Only say this, however, if you really mean it. There's no point in waiting until the door shuts behind your guests to start huffing that they've drunk your best whisky or ruined your sound system/kitchen knives/life. Try, as far as possible, to pre-empt their needs by showing them where to find clean towels, toiletries, teabags etc.

It breaks every rule of hospitality if visitors are made to feel like they're a nuisance. Especially if they are.

DINNER PARTIES

Having friends round for dinner is a congenial and informal way of announcing your new *ménage* to your circle. If you are both used to entertaining single-handedly, it is a good idea to define areas of responsibility, playing to your respective strengths. Some 'strengths' are more enjoyable than others. Your partner may be a whizz with a dish mop. This does not mean she wishes to spend the entire evening at the sink while you relax and enjoy your guests' company.

If you're of the 'take us as you find us' school of entertaining and your girlfriend prefers a more managed affair, go with her instincts. This is your chance to show off the home you have created together, so a bit of art direction will do no harm. Fresh flowers and plumped upholstery strike the balance between making an effort and staging a major production. Arranging coffee-table books/magazines for effect is trying too hard.

A glass of champagne or good sparkling wine to welcome your guests will hit a celebratory note. You may wish to offer pre-prandial spirits (gin/vodka/Martini) or you can stick to wine or beer. While your guests will probably bring a bottle, it appears a little desperate if you're waiting, corkscrew in hand, for the offering, so have a red and a white already opened (there is an argument for serving your best wines first, while guests are in a state to appreciate it). If someone brings a particularly fine vintage, it is appropriate to share it with the company, but this can be done, with appropriate ceremony, later in the evening.

Even if there is no formal table plan, you should have given some thought to where guests will sit before they arrive at the table. Boy/girl/boy is not strictly necessary, but couples should not, as a rule, be seated together. If the table is very large or there are discernible 'cold spots', you can always change places before pudding. In the event that a guest is unhappily placed (e.g. next to a thundering bore or 'hands on' lech) you can find some friendly pretext to swap seats with the victim without upsetting the whole table.

The manly skill of carving, though impressive, is no longer de rigueur in a host. If you feel you're going to mess it up, by all means go at the joint with an electric carving knife in the kitchen, or ask a more qualified guest to help.

It is, however, your job, as host, to direct the conversation, or at least set a few broadly inclusive balls rolling. If talk strays into areas that are uncomfortable for anyone at the table, you should intervene; it is better to cut short an opinionated or aggressive individual than to risk real offence to another guest in your home.

If your partner has done most of the cooking, it is appropriate (and indeed politic) to compliment her. If the meal is an unqualified disaster, it is not your place to draw attention to it. Remember that the most memorable dinner parties are not always, or even usually, *cordon bleu* affairs.

Whatever happens, your newly united front as co-hosts should hold until the last guest has departed. It is the height of bad manners to criticise your partner's efforts in front of guests. It won't do you a whole lot of good behind closed doors, either.

THROWING A PARTY

'Let's have a party!' It's one of those ideas which occurs about half way down the wine bottle, when you're feeling snuggly in your nest. If you're still enthused in the morning, you need to bat the idea back and forth between you until a clear shape for the event emerges. Wine or cocktails? Evening drinks or all-night bash with dancing? Structure is key, because the last thing you want to encourage in your new home is a studenty free-for-all.

If you or your partner are on the retentive side of houseproud, and fear for your carpets and soft furnishings, you might consider a discreet ban on red wine; you can placate guests who turn up with an indifferent bottle of Chianti by scanning the label with evident rapture and insisting it must be put away for some more worthy occasion. While guests may see through this polite fiction, they are unlikely to

insist, for their part, that the bottle is just cheap plonk.

Guest lists need to be agreed with your partner. While your rugby club mates may mesh perfectly with her book club girls, factions should not dominate. Nor should you lose your head on the day of the party because not enough people have RSVP'd and run round inviting everyone in your office/pub/street (as a rule of thumb for big parties, you can expect about twice as many guests as official responses).

Forward planning should take care of food and drink supplies and it is a good idea to have a playlist of suitable music lined up. If, on the appointed evening, you skulk in the office or remember an important meeting, leaving your girlfriend to rush about like a mad person pushing back sofas and setting out nuts, do not expect to be met at the door with a welcoming drink.

When the house is thronged with people, it helps if one you is wine waiter while the other keeps an eye out for social casualties. It's possible that you or your partner are the only person some guests know, so it's up to you to effect introductions.

If heated arguments break out, it's the host's responsibility to diffuse the tension and, if necessary, eject belligerent parties. Medical casualties can usually be averted if spotted early enough; the very drunk should be steered towards the garden on grounds of 'needing air' (you don't want your bathroom out of commission).

In the event of accidental spillages/breakages, the host should clear up quickly, efficiently and without fuss; offers to pay for the damage should be waved away. If the guilty party turns up in the next few days with a replacement item, accept the gift graciously (even if it's not half as nice as the original). It is always bad form, however, to pursue guests in your home with bills for costs incurred.

Even if your guests behave with the aplomb of extras in a Noel Coward play, you may eventually need to signal the end of the festivities when it gets too late. This is a good sign – think how unsettling it would be if the house were cleared and the glasses washed by 10 pm.

Slowing drinks to a respectable trickle usually gets the message across; it is rude to come over like a stroppy landlord and 'switch off' the alcohol supply after a certain hour, but you can circulate with freshly brewed coffee as an alternative.

It is never acceptable, no matter how late the hour, for the host to retire, leaving his guests to 'get on with it'. You must both sit it out until the very last guest leaves. Take the liberty of calling cabs/arranging lifts for stragglers and be prepared to offer a bed to anyone incapable of getting home.

As co-hosts, it is pointless apportioning blame at the post-mortem stage ('why did you invite so-and-so', 'was that my single malt you were ladling into that old soak?'). If you and your house are still standing, your party was a success. Savour the moment.

GRAND GESTURES

Presents are the milestones of relationships. It's a racing certainty that anniversaries, birthdays and so on are more important to your girlfriend than they are to you.

Accept that you cannot keep up with the ever growing list of festivals to be marked (half-anniversary of making-up-after-first-argument etc.), but observing important occasions with a thoughtfully chosen present will rack up your credit. If you have difficulty remembering dates, set up an electronic alert on your laptop or mobile phone.

With women (the nice ones, at any rate), it really is the thought that counts. Anything that shows a bit of effort and imagination will be a hit and, if you don't run to imagination, you can rely on thorough research. The aim is to find a gift that 'speaks' clearly and directly to the girl. If you have shared tastes in books or music, choosing exactly the right volume or album will emphasise that closeness; if it's a hard-to-find edition, so much the better.

If your partner is a woman of decided tastes, and they happen to be tastes you cannot fathom, you need to seek expert guidance from friends, sisters or knowledgeable sales assistants. The dedicated follower of fashion will be thrilled with this season's 'must-have' accessory (handbag/sunglasses etc.) and the fact that you normally couldn't tell a Gucci from a hole in the ground will only increase the gift's sentimental value.

Jewellery is the most traditional love-token, but needs to be chosen with care. Rings are dicey near the beginning of a relationship as they may be 'read' the wrong way. Bracelets are generally less often worn than necklaces or earrings (check whether her ears are pierced). Above all, the jewellery should fit with pieces she already owns. Does she go for delicate or chunky, contemporary or classic? Most women favour a particular metal (gold/silver). These preferences need to be checked out before you make your purchase.

Lingerie, too, can be a minefield. Rifle through her knicker drawer to get her exact size (be certain to look at more than one pair) – it knocks the glamour off the gift if she can't struggle into it. If you are too bashful or bewildered to buy underwear, a drop dead gorgeous nightie will strike the right note of intimate luxury. When it comes to style, err on the side of tasteful and rely on quality (i.e. price) to provide the 'wow' factor. If she really liked scarlet, tasselled undergarments, she'd have a drawerful by now. The same goes for anything in leather with more than the usual complement of holes.

It's a very rare woman who doesn't appreciate flowers. Roses (long-stemmed) are the classic emblem of romance. If cost is an issue, one perfect, exotic bloom (orchid, amaryllis etc.) will have more impact than a mixed bunch from a petrol station. Supermarkets now sell perfectly lovely flowers. It only takes two minutes to remove the price-stickered cellophane sheaths, and a classy ribbon or length of twine will elevate the bunch to boutique status. Carnations, chrysanthemums and lilies are associated, in some cultures, with death, so unless you know your girlfriend has a particular penchant for these flowers, they are best avoided.

If your girlfriend has such exacting taste that you daren't risk choosing a gift, you can always go for the 'spoiling' option – book her in for a 'personal shopping' appointment with vouchers to spend at her favourite store or arrange a day at a top-quality spa with some special pampering treatments.

Nicest of all, particularly if you don't have as much time together as you'd like, squeeze some space from your diary (and hers, which may require covert collaboration with her boss/family/friends) and surprise her with a weekend away. If she's the one who generally runs your social life, a surprise birthday dinner organised by you and attended by her closest friends will be a real treat – all the more so as it is a public declaration of how much you care about her.

Some women baulk at the idea of 'practical' gifts, but it's not a hard and fast rule. A keen cook may be thrilled with a state-of-the-art food processor, a technophile may love the latest mobile phone. The only real pitfall is the present that looks suspiciously like something you wanted for yourself – few feminine hearts will leap as the wrapping falls away from a floor-sander or computerised rowing machine.

On the wrapping front, it's nice if you've made an effort, or if the shop has made a professional job of the presentation, but most women will not expect unrealistic levels of artistry – just make sure you've fished the receipt out of the carrier bag. What does matter, however, is the accompanying card, as this is likely to be laid by for posterity. An original and heartfelt message, appropriate to the occasion, is a surefire way of making 'the thought that counted' count that little bit more.

MAINTAINING STANDARDS

It's by no means a given that the comforts of living together should turn to complacency, but it can happen.

It's hard to keep up the allure when you're endlessly available. Of course half the point of moving in together was to see more of each other, but a degree of autonomy is vital. Don't ditch your old social life, because your girlfriend almost certainly won't want to ditch hers and one-sided deals necessarily breed resentment. While we don't want to feel that you're finding excuses to stay out of the house, we will worry if you have no life beyond the relationship. We may crave the satisfaction of coming first in your life, but if there's nothing to come before, the victory can feel a little hollow.

Success lies in never treating each other like the default entertainment. If you have arranged to spend the evening together – even if you're just slobbing out on the sofa with a takeaway – it's dismissive (and suggests your time is at a higher premium than hers) to cancel if you get a more exciting offer.

Nobody needs – or wants – to be on their best behaviour all the time, but that doesn't mean you should stop trying to impress. It does nothing for the self-confidence of either party if you only make an effort when you're going out.

Most women do not expect full-on princess treatment, but the occasional bunch of flowers or breakfast in bed (not just on designated festivals) will remind us of the prince who wooed us. A shared wheelie bin need not put the kibosh on romance.

Remember that living together need not altogether rule out spontaneous passion. A kiss is still a kiss. A sigh is still a sigh. The fundamental things remain – and the rest just keeps getting better.

THE NEXT STEP

I t is only when the first rush subsides and rings of dancing cupids make their bow that a couple really starts to know each other. Personal habits come to the fore and not all of them are enticing. Issues of compatibility and commitment pop up and refuse to pop down again.

Holding your nerve at this critical time in the relationship is easier if you keep a sense of humour. Celebrating the good stuff shouldn't stop just because there are important decisions to be made.

When you're saying goodbye to the single life it helps to remember that commitment isn't a threat, it's a promise.

COMMUNICATION

There is nothing modern men like more than sitting down for a really good chin-wag about their relationship. Only joking. Most men would rather stick pins in their eyes than disclose the state of their affairs. Nine times out of ten, when a man says 'I want to talk about our relationship' he means – and we know that he means – 'the relationship is over'.

Women, on the other hand, talk to their friends, to people they barely know and are especially keen to talk to you. They confide the ins and outs (yup, 'fraid so, boys) of their love life to their friends, to their neighbours, to their cat… This difference in genetic disposition is what frustrates effective communication between the sexes. Put more bluntly, this is what frustrates women. Can you think of an occasion when a male friend complained that his other half wouldn't 'open up' to him? No? Well take it on trust. Women do this all the time.

The good news, given the general reticence of men in this regard, is that it's fantastically easy to appear emotionally articulate. The simple substitution of 'I feel' for 'I think' in any given sentence is a good start and, if you find the idea of laying bare your own feelings just too alarming at this stage in the relationship, then asking your partner what she feels comes a very creditable second.

If your partner is in an unexplained huff, 'tell me what you're feeling' goes a lot further than 'what's up with you?'. It is important that you listen to the answer and de-code where necessary. 'I loved it when we used to kiss at bus-stops', for example, is woman-speak for 'Get off your undemonstrative a*** and show me some affection'.

If you are the kind of man who cannot talk about your own or anyone else's feelings, under any circumstances, you can still be a good listener. If, say, your partner needs to talk about a sensitive issue (e.g. the death or illness of a friend or family member), it's no good throwing up your hands and saying 'I'm not good with these things'. Wordless sympathy can be sincere, especially if backed up by physical closeness.

Good communication is particularly important when you are often apart. Phone manners can make or break a long distance relationship and the phone calls (or most of them) should be proper conversations, not just a means of managing the practicalities of the relationship. At the very least, we will expect the television to be turned off and a modicum of privacy when you call us. Concentrate on what we're saying; there'll be extra marks for the man who remembers how we were feeling the last time we spoke.

Whether phoning or face to face, some things just have to be verbalised. If you choke on the words 'I love you', you need to practise more because your partner (if that is indeed what you wish her to be) needs to hear it more than you probably realise, and not just on anniversaries and Valentine's Day. Giving her a card with the words already printed on it is not the same. If you really can't say it, then write it down, but avoid clichés and glib formulations ('I love you', by the way, is not a cliché, it's a classic).

'Lots of love' is a perfectly suitable sign-off for mothers, sisters and retiring secretaries. Your girlfriend will expect something a little more personal.

HOW TO HANDLE US

Deep down, every woman is waiting for her soulmate – the one person on this earth who understands us perfectly and knows what we're thinking before we've articulated it ourselves. Maybe it's this tantalising illusion of perfection that makes us a little ratty now and then when our real, fallible loves forget to bring home chocolate when we've been thinking about it really hard, or fail to notice our haircut.

Once the rosy flush of passion has subsided, a certain amount of arguing is inevitable, and can even be constructive; the trick is to save it for things that really matter. Arguments start to go badly wrong when you stray from the agenda: keep to the issue in hand and resist the temptation to bring up old grievances.

If the downward spiral is gaining momentum, call an adjournment. Tell your girlfriend you're not discussing things further for the moment and that you will resume negotiations when you are both feeling calmer; as long as they *are* resumed and this is not just an avoidance tactic, we will (probably) be grateful for the opportunity to 'rein back' before things are said that we both regret.

If regrettable things do slip out, apologise at once – and again later – if you feel that the first apology evaporated in the heat of the moment. If you're the one being apologised to, accept it graciously and don't turn the apology into Stage Two of the argument. Sulking, in either sex, is deeply unattractive.

Don't be too alarmed by tears. For most women, it's a natural release; let us get it out of our system and offer the manly shoulder. There's nothing wrong with men crying either, but it's probably best saved for moments of deep emotion rather than the passing beauty of the sunset.

If you suspect 'crocodile tears', shed purely for effect, keep a private log of her mood swings. Over time a pattern will usually become apparent – if your girlfriend regularly weeps or resorts to hysterical threats to get her own way, you can either point out (gently and humorously, if possible) that she's been rumbled, or you can frustrate the whole exercise by refusing to react.

Real women, of course, will not resort to these manipulative tactics and will be unimpressed if you are unduly swayed by others (mothers, sisters, ex girlfriends, friends) who do. It is also worth noting that often we will be aware of these tactics before you are.

Laughter, for some men – particularly if they haven't grown up with sisters – is almost as alarming as tears, but it's something else that women do all the time. We may be laughing with you, quite often we'll be laughing at you; it doesn't mean we don't love and respect you. If you are genuinely wounded and made to feel uncomfortable by an over-hilarious woman, explain your feelings. Otherwise, just laugh back – you may never know what is quite so funny, but it will still feel good.

JEALOUSY

No modern woman likes to feel like a chattel. Cave-man jealousy is a hugely destructive emotion; it makes us feel smothered, rather than loved.

It really isn't necessary to know exactly what your partner is doing/who she is speaking to every minute of the day. Nor should you feel accountable in this regard. Insecurity breeds mistrust, and if you can't trust us we will start to wonder why you have chosen to be with us in the first place.

Some forms of jealousy are mere macho posturing, and some women – though by no means the majority – rather like it. There's nothing wrong with 'claiming' your girlfriend in a social group ('the lady's with me') but make it an affectionate, rather than an aggressive, gesture. If your girlfriend flirts wildly with another man in front of you, it may be a bid for attention and, as such, is easily dealt with; just make her feel as attractive as he does. If you're disinclined to gallantry in this situation, you can employ the simple, but brutally effective, technique of pretending not to notice.

When social flirting starts to trigger 'after hours' quarrels, however, you need to lay down some ground rules. Raise the subject without making too big a deal of it – a larky reminder before going out is better than recriminations after the event – and ask your girlfriend to tone it down. Remember, though, that some flirting is entirely one-sided. It's not our fault if some old lech engages in deep and meaningful conversation with our chest. If we're not bothered, let it go. Remarks along the lines of 'I told you not to wear that dress' rarely improve matters.

Sustained jealousy of a particular 'rival' is harder to deal with. If you're uncomfortable about our close relationship with a male friend, it is perfectly reasonable to suggest limits (no late night *tête a têtes* or staying over at his house). Any reasonable woman will put herself in your situation and agree terms without huffing or high drama.

The territorial rage some men feel vis à vis their partner's ex boyfriends is a frequent cause of real unhappiness, but think about it: your partner could not be faithful to you before she met you and there is some good reason why she is not with this person now. The actual threat he presents is therefore negatively rated. In rational terms, you've more cause to be jealous of the milkman.

Whatever the problem, possessiveness is never the solution. A healthy relationship is not about the closing down of options, but the opening up of new, shared horizons. Geoffrey Chaucer was definitely onto something when he wrote 'Love is a thing as any spirit free/and will not be constrained by mastery'. Just don't quote him at 2 am and expect a polite response.

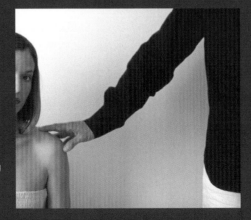

ALL YOUR FAULT

There are certain things a man should never do or say. They're not all deal-breakers, but no good can ever come of...

Commenting on what we eat: even if we have bored you rigid with the details of our diet and our determination to stick thereto and you're trying to be helpful, it is pointless to warn us off that particular bar of chocolate as there will be a very good reason for us eating it.

Enquiring whether it's 'that time of the month' when we appear a little snappish. Especially if you know it is.

Forgetting the names of all our friends, but expecting us to remember the names and professions of all yours.

Starting sentences with 'I don't mean to be critical, but...'.

Becoming financially dependent on us; it's just not sexy.

Taking longer to get ready and get out than we do.

Fretting about your appearance. The only thing worse is fretting about ours.

Criticising our driving when you're too drunk to drive yourself.

Asking 'isn't she great?' about a female friend or colleague and expecting us to like her.

Letting us tidy up after you, and then pleading that it's not mess, it's lifestyle.

The ritual omission of two/three glasses when the washing up finally gets done.

Imitating our voice when, in the middle of an argument, we go a bit squeaky.

Laughing at our 'faddy' foods, then coming home drunk and eating them just the same.

Stealing our best stories.

ALL OUR FAULT

It will have become apparent, in the course of your relationship, that the female mind occasionally transcends the rational. There's nothing you – or we – can do about this, but it may help you to know that we're aware of the problem.

We know, deep in our reptile consciousness, that there are certain situations that no man, however adroit, sensitive or well-meaning, can successfully negotiate. These include:

Asking if you have noticed our wrinkles. This is a trap question and there is no correct answer (the unwary swain will plump for 'no' and provoke a 40-minute diatribe on how it's all very well for men to look characterful, etc.).

Expecting you to pinpoint one reason out of a possible 300 why we're upset ('if you don't know what you've done, there's no point my telling you…').

Our ability to calculate compound interest on ancient grievances.

Demanding to know whether you find that woman over there attractive and sulking when you say 'yes'.

Complaining that you never do housework, then complaining more when you don't do it right (i.e. the way our mother taught us).

Our tendency to nag you about perceived shortcomings, even though we know they are written on the male DNA. These include:

The inability to multi-task ('what do you mean I'm standing there doing nothing? I'm making a list').

A constitutional lack of interest in other people's relationships ('they seem happy enough to me…').

Problems with deferred gratification (beer now, washing up later).

We know this stuff is not your fault. It doesn't mean we like it.

FINISHING IT

So it's just not working out. Fabulous fling or *folie à deux*, a significant relationship (one lasting, say, six months or more) deserves to be closed with some ceremony.

It is a cop-out, and plain rude, to finish with someone you have been close to over the phone; indeed the only thing worse is the 'digital dump', where the bad news arrives by text or email.

If you are the one calling time on the relationship, the onus is on you to be kind. However difficult the conversation may be for you, it will be significantly worse for the dumpee so she deserves every consideration. It is not very kind to prolong a moribund relationship. If you're sure you want to end it, it is best to bite the bullet and break the news as soon as possible.

If however, your girlfriend is under temporary stress from other quarters (imminent exams, family/work crisis) it is chivalrous to 'take the strain' until the rest of her life is in order. Nor should you let her know that you have been 'waiting for the right moment', as this serves only to taint good memories.

Whatever happens, your girlfriend should be the first to hear your decision; it heaps humiliation upon horror if your entire mutual acquaintance knows of your disaffection before she does. There are better ways of preparing the ground. 'We need to talk' is universal code for 'I'm not happy with the way things are going', but it's cruel to send out this signal without following through fast.

Privacy is always preferable for difficult conversations. Her home is better than yours, as you can leave when you feel there is nothing useful left to be said. Choosing a restaurant or wine bar may lessen the odds of histrionics, but it's still a risky strategy with potential for embarrassment all round; whatever the background to the break-up, any man walking out on a tearful woman will appear irredeemably caddish. If you have plumped for a public dismissal, decency demands that you pay any bills and see the lady home (or at least find her a cab).

When it comes to your reasons for finishing, tell the truth. But maybe not the whole truth. 'I don't feel that I can offer the kind of commitment you deserve' is much better than 'I cannot stand another hour in your needy, hysterical clutches'. It is entirely likely that any personal criticisms (and however you phrase it, it will necessarily feel like criticism) will be met with a counterblast detailing your own egregious failings. Roll, if you can, with the punches. Point scoring, at this stage in the game, hardly matters.

If you're breaking up because you've found someone else, say so – the shock to your partner will be less painful than weeks of wondering where it all went wrong. On top of which, your new romance is bound to 'come out' sooner or later and you will look like a weasel for concealing it.

If you are the one on the receiving end of the break-up, you've every right to expect these courtesies from your partner. Listen carefully to her reasons; if you feel she is mounting an unfair case for the prosecution, say so, but don't waste too much time applying logic to lost love. If it is clear that she has made up her mind, thank her for the good times and leave. This may require a superhuman act of will, but you will (eventually) feel better for keeping your dignity.

An affirmative is the only polite response to 'Can we still be friends?'. This does not mean that you can or should be endlessly available to each other in the aftermath of the split. In fact it's probably kinder to keep a bit of distance until the emotional fallout has dispersed. Nor should you be seen whooping it up round town, with or without a new lover in tow. The end of love is a passing, and a period of mourning – or at least public observance of such – is seemly.

COMMITMENT

It's all going terribly well. You're finishing each other's sentences and laughing at each other's jokes (even though you've heard them three times already) and before you know it the C-word crops up. Commitment. A big scary abstract noun with the power to reduce grown men to gibbering wrecks. It's not that you don't love your girlfriend, it's certainly not that you want to be with anyone else, it's just, well, you know, commitment…

So what does it actually mean? It means, among other things, growing up. It means sorting out priorities and making choices. It means a radical shift in perspective from 'me' to 'us'. The fear, for a lot of men, is that it means the end of fun.

The fear is natural. It is human nature to jib at fences. And if you view commitment purely as a restriction on your freedom, then you're probably not quite ready for it. An unhurried list of pros and cons may, however, increase the appeal.

On the 'con' side, it indubitably means saying goodbye to your single lifestyle. And this is something you need to think hard about. A lot will depend on your age. Look around you – are your friends still largely out there, dating an unending stream of women and crashing at each other's pads after a night on the booze? Or are they gradually pairing off and setting up homes with baby alarms and lawnmowers? It may well be that the single life you enjoyed together has said goodbye to you.

Even if you feel that age is not an issue for you, it will almost certainly be an issue for your partner if she hopes to have a family. If there are certain ambitions you or your partner wish to achieve before marriage/children, it will be useful to set a clear time frame. If, on the other hand, you are flatly appalled by the whole idea of 2.4 domesticity, then now is the time to say so.

Biological clocks aside, men and women mature at different rates. The odds on a simultaneous desire to commit are remote. If instinct tells you that your aspirations will converge more closely in the future, give yourselves some breathing space before rushing into any life-changing decisions. But if you or your partner cannot convincingly imagine yourself into a happy shared existence, then you need to consider that the relationship may be fundamentally flawed. Certainly moving in together/marriage never made a bad relationship better.

You'll know the time is right for commitment when you feel lucky and excited about this new stage in your life, when the sense of momentum is irresistible. 'Going steady' has its charms. The future should feel like an adventure.

HOW TO PROPOSE

For all but the most impetuously romantic, a proposal requires planning. It's an occasion you'll be telling your children about, so you want to get it right.

Pick a location that holds special memories for you both. Or, if you can afford it, go for no holds barred, once in a lifetime romance – the top of the Empire State, a hot air balloon over the Kalahari – this is a moment when you deserve to be stars in your own movie.

Timing is everything. However meticulous your planning, it is possible that you will be overtaken by events. If your girlfriend has chosen that evening to pick a fight over who was supposed to collect the dry cleaning, it might be worth delaying as she may not wish her fabulous bolshiness to be part of the memory. On the other hand, nothing lightens a lady's mood like a diamond… it's your call, but aim to be flexible.

Enlisting the help of friends/head waiters etc. in your masterplan is always risky (what if she says 'no'?), but if you're sure of her response and think she'd enjoy the spotlight, by all means rope them in.

While it's not obligatory to go down on one knee – some may find it corny – most women will love it. There's something rather nice too, about the traditional form of words ('Mary Jones, will you do me the honour…') though when it comes right down to it, there can be no truly offensive way of asking someone to marry you.

Just do what you're comfortable with, but remember to listen to the answer. She may need a moment to take it all in. If she needs more than a moment, it's not a great sign. If she says 'no', and you're genuinely shocked by the answer, it's not your job to make her feel better about it. It's as well to have a response up your sleeve to cover what is bound to be an excruciating moment for you both. If you have already presented the ring, she should offer to give it back. Whether you take it or not is up to you.

In the happier and statistically much more likely event of her accepting, a Hollywood kiss and copious champagne is in order. Tell those that matter – a phone call to parents and best friends will suffice – and then relish the moment.

It is not strictly necessary to have the engagement ring about your person when you propose, but some kind of pledge – such as a small piece of jewellery – is appropriate. Or, you could propose with a diamond and then choose the setting together.

If your new fiancée is a lady of exacting taste, she may well consider it more romantic if you choose the rock and the ring together at a later date. That, in any case, will be her line, and the happiest of men will surely not object.

BUYING A DIAMOND

Anyone who hasn't bought a diamond before will be shocked at the price. As a rule of thumb, you can expect to pay the jeweller up to twice your monthly salary. You can find some beautiful antique rings at slightly lower prices, but women can be superstitious about pre-owned love tokens, so it's as well to do some subtle 'fishing' first.

If you want to surprise your fiancée with 'the perfect ring', but are unsure of her taste (or, for that matter, yours), you could enlist the help of one of her girlfriends – just make sure it's a friend whose style your fiancée admires.

Whether you're buying the ring alone, with guidance or with your fiancée herself, it can only add to your man-about-town allure if you know what you're looking for. 'The Four Cs' are your watchwords – cut, clarity, colour and carat.

The cut describes the shape of the stone. A rectangular diamond is known, confusingly, as an 'emerald cut', the square shape is a 'princess cut' and a triangle is a 'trillion'. A 'pear shape' stone, provokingly for pedants, more closely resembles a teardrop. Cut has little bearing on price, but many engagement rings favour round stones (the classic 'brilliant cut') as this shape offers the best 'flash factor'.

Clarity in diamonds is graded from the extremely rare and expensive IF (internally flawless) through a minutely calibrated scale of flaws or 'inclusions' ranging from VS1 (very slightly included category 1) to 13 (imperfect). While the amount of inclusions determine the price, they need not detract greatly from the beauty of the stone. A solitaire (single diamond) in the 'slightly or very slightly included' categories is still a high quality piece of jewellery.

Colour in diamonds can go two ways. A slight trace of brown, yellow or grey brings down the price, while stones with a deep, even colour are rare and therefore more expensive. Colour is graded alphabetically, with anything up to H considered 'white'. Most stones sold for engagement rings will be H grade or above.

'Carat' is the glamorous term for a diamond's weight. The bigger the stone, the heavier the carat weight and, consequently, the heavier the price tag. One carat is a very respectable size for a solitaire.

Your research may impress upon the jeweller that you aren't an utter novice in the diamond buying field, but expect to be bamboozled by further specialist information, as the scope for discrimination is endless. At the end of the day, a decent sized stone in a relatively simple and classic setting is likely to hit the mark, but it is prudent to make sure the ring can be exchanged if necessary. And if you divine a fleeting trace of disappointment in your fiancée's face when you present the ring, offer a swap immediately and cheerfully. She will probably be most embarrassed but, if you insist, she will be grateful every day of her life.

'An excellent wife,' the book of Proverbs reminds us, 'has a price beyond jewels.' Don't let the wrong diamond come between you and your best investment.

P.S...

BEST MAN AND USHER

BEST MAN
This is a major role requiring high levels of diplomacy, confidence and reliability.

You must work discreetly and efficiently to ensure that the day runs smoothly; you will be the first point of contact if there is a crisis.

THE BEST MAN'S DUTIES INCLUDE:
Arranging a stag night or weekend at least several weeks in advance of the wedding.

Making sure the ushers have the correct clothes and know what is expected of them.

Familiarising yourself with the ceremony and reception venues and the timetable of events.

Staying with the groom the night before.

Checking that you/the groom have everything you need (not forgetting the rings).

Accompanying the groom to the ceremony venue in good time (at least 45 minutes in advance) and reassuring him if he is nervous.

Looking out for a nod from the chief usher to say that the bride has arrived and handing over the ring(s) at the critical moment.

Ensuring that the bride and groom are ready to have their photographs taken; getting them into the car (or equivalent) that will take them to the reception.

Having money ready if any payments (e.g. for the church or band) are required on the day.

Delivering your speech. Don't drink too much until the speeches are over.

Ensuring that the first night/honeymoon luggage (and tickets and passports) are in the correct vehicle.

Making sure that guests leave the reception safely and sorting out taxis if necessary.

USHERS
Good friends or relatives are usually chosen to be ushers, who on the day are floor managers, crowd controllers and general helpers.

Before the big day, the ushers' only duties are to ensure that they have a suitable outfit to wear and to attend the stag night.

THE USHERS' DUTIES INCLUDE:
Collecting buttonholes/service sheets.

Arriving at the ceremony venue at least 45 minutes in advance.

Handing out the order of service sheets to guests when they arrive and leading them to their seats (bride's family on the right, groom's family on the left (viewed from the back).

If the venue is filling up on one side and not the other, ensuring the crowd is balanced out.

Letting guests know, on arrival, about any photographic or confetti restrictions.

Escorting the groom's parents and the mother of the bride to their seats.

Ensuring that guests move from the ceremony to the reception efficiently.

At the reception, helping guests find their tables.

THE GODFATHER

Being chosen to be a godfather is a great honour. Traditionally, a child has three godparents; a boy one godmother and two godfathers and a girl one godfather and two godmothers. Now it is fashionable in some circles to have several godparents; the mix may vary irrespective of the sex of the child.

INITIAL DUTIES:
At the christening, you will be expected to stand with the parents and other godparents at the font as the baby is anointed. You will have to read (from the order of service) a few words in answer to the ordinand's questions about your willingness to be a guide and support to the child.

A christening present is expected; confer with the other godparents to make sure you don't double up. Parents will understand if you are not financially capable of giving a traditional silver napkin ring or laying down a case of vintage port; instead, buy something that the baby will enjoy now, and save the showy gifts for later on.

A suitable gift for a baby girl is a charm bracelet that you add to each birthday, or a photo album in which you or her parents can chart her life.

For a baby boy, you could open a savings bond – they will enjoy receiving an annual statement and seeing their nest egg grow.

ONGOING OBLIGATIONS:
Never forget a birthday, Christmas or other significant date.

Try to be there occasionally for sports days, school plays, graduation. Do not steal their parents' thunder, but your godchild (and their parents) will appreciate and notice your effort to be part of their life.

Find ways of keeping in touch at other times. When you go away on trips, send a postcard. If you see something in a magazine that might amuse or interest them, cut it out and send it to them.

Spend time with your godchild alone. Do things that interest them and give their parents a break; that way you make friends with the child and return them happy to refreshed and grateful parents.

Give them interesting rather than expensive gifts – an unusual trinket from a foreign trip will be more memorable than the latest electronic game or gadget.

If you have several godchildren, try and get them together now and again, so providing them with a ready-made circle of contacts and support for later life.

Never criticise or undermine their parents: your job is to help the child understand its parents' position and provide wise advice on how to deal with it, not to side with the child or deepen any existing rifts.

When they are old enough, give your godchild your phone number and let them feel that they can call you at any time.

Speak to them as your equal; you have a unique opportunity to be one of their first grown-up friends who won't judge or nag them, and with whom they can share their fears and doubts without looking silly.

LETTER-WRITING

THANK YOU LETTERS
Should be written if you have spent the night/weekend with someone, or attended an event they have hosted.

Write on good quality unlined writing paper (white, ivory or cream is preferable).

The form of invitation dictates the formality of the thank you letter; cards or postcards are acceptable if the event was less formal, or the invitation extended by phone or email (in which case an email thank you is fine).

Thank yous should be posted within 7–10 days of the event – the sooner the better.

Gifts should also be promptly acknowledged with a thank you letter.

REPLIES TO AN 'AT HOME' INVITATION
An 'At Home' is the traditional form for an invitation to a private event such as a lunch, supper, reception or cocktail party.

The reply should be a handwritten letter, addressed solely to the hostess on the envelope, and traditionally written in the third person without salutation/signature (e.g. 'Mr Joseph Jones thanks Mrs Christopher Smith for her kind invitation to dinner on the 3rd July and looks forward to attending').

If an email address/phone number is given, it is acceptable to reply through these media.

If the invitation is to you 'and Guest', the reply should specify the name of the guest you're bringing. If the invitation is to you and a named partner, only substitute a different guest after checking with the hostess.

REPLYING TO WEDDING INVITATIONS
Address the hostess on the envelope, but refer to both of the bride's parents (or other hosts on the invitation) inside. Replies should be sent promptly upon receipt.

Write in the third person, without salutation or signature.

The date should be written at the bottom of the page.

All elements of the invitation are repeated (e.g. 'Mr James Watts thanks Mr and Mrs Brown for the kind invitation to the marriage of their daughter Emma, to Mr Henry Wright, at All Saints Church, Brampton, on Saturday 7th July at 3 o'clock and afterwards at The Vicarage, and is delighted to accept/regrets that he is unable to attend.').

LETTERS OF CONDOLENCE
Letters should be written promptly on hearing of the bereavement.

They should be handwritten on proper writing paper or a blank greetings card (avoid 'With Sympathy' cards) and posted first class or hand-delivered.

They should be carefully thought out, and appropriate to your relationship with the deceased's family.

Expressions of 'knowing exactly how they feel' are rarely well-accepted, but a brief anecdote or fond memory of the deceased is ideal.

Do not not expect a response; the individual will decide whether he/she feels able to reply.

DRESS CODES

WHITE TIE (OR 'EVENING DRESS')

The most formal, and rare, of dress codes, worn in the evening for royal ceremonies and balls. It may also be specified for formal evening weddings. The regimental equivalent is 'Mess Dress' or 'Mess Uniform'.

- Black tail coat (the shape is different to a morning coat – don't confuse the two).
- Matching black trousers with two lines of braid down each outside leg.
- White shirt with detachable wing collar, cufflinks and studs (these come in sets of four, are usually black onyx, and fit through four holes in the shirt-front like tiny cufflinks).
- Thin white marcella bow-tie and white marcella evening waistcoat.
- Black patent lace-up shoes/black silk socks.

BLACK TIE (OR 'DINNER JACKETS')

- Black wool dinner jacket with silk lapels (peaked/curved), no vents, covered buttons.
- Black trousers with a slight taper and ideally cut for braces, with one row of braid.
- White evening shirt in cotton or silk with a marcella or pleated front and a soft turn-down collar, black studs and cufflinks.
- A black (ideally silk) bow-tie.
- Cummerbands can be worn, but a low cut black evening waistcoat is preferable.
- Black lace-up shoes and black socks.

MORNING DRESS (OR 'FORMAL DAY DRESS')

Traditional dress for weddings and formal daytime events in the presence of The Queen (e.g. Ascot, Trooping the Colour).

The morning coat – black or grey is fine – has curved front edges sloping back at the sides into long tails. It is single-breasted with one button, and usually has peaked lapels.

Although grey is the traditional colour for a waistcoat under a black morning coat, patterned or coloured waistcoats are also acceptable. Single-breasted waistcoats should be worn with the bottom button undone, double-breasted with all buttons fastened. Avoid backless waistcoats as you will not be able remove your morning coat.

Trousers should be grey with a grey morning coat, or grey and black striped (or grey houndstooth) with a black coat.

Morning dress should be worn with a plain white shirt with stiff turn-down collar, double-cuffs and appropriate cufflinks.

The tie or cravat is traditionally of heavy woven silk. Black or silver is traditional, but non-garish pastels are frequently worn.

Formal black shoes should be lace-up and highly polished.

Grey felt hats are optional at most weddings (except for the groom/his men) and should be carried rather than worn inside church. They are obligatory for the Royal Enclosure at Ascot and must be worn at all times.

LOUNGE SUITS

A lounge suit is a normal business suit worn with a shirt and tie.

They are worn on less formal occasions, such as an early evening drinks party, when you are arriving straight from work/the City. They are also acceptable for weddings.

Smart black shoes should be worn but need not be lace-ups.

TYING TIES

STANDARD 'FOUR-IN-HAND' KNOT
Suitable for men with shorter necks, as the rather narrow and elongated form of the knot stretches the perceived height of the neck:

- Button the collar and lift it, draping the tie around the neck with wider end on your right, hanging slightly lower than the narrow end.

- Cross the wide end over the narrow end and wind around twice, looping up through the neck hole on the second time around.

- Push the wide end down through the knot and tug gently until tight. The wide tip should finish just below the stomach, more or less even with, and covering, the narrow end.

WINDSOR KNOT
- Button the collar and lift it, draping the tie around the neck with the wider end on your right, hanging about 12 inches below the narrow end.

- Cross the wide end over the narrow end and instead of winding right round, bring the wide end up through the neck loop, then down to the left, and underneath the narrow end to the right.

- Pull the wide end up back through the loop (from front to back) and out to the right again (the wide end will be inside out).

- Bring the wide end across the front from right to left, then up through the loop once more. Bring the wide end down through the knot in front and tighten the knot carefully, drawing it up to the collar.

A REAL BOW TIE
It's easier to tie a bow tie on someone else, rather than tying it yourself. If you have enlisted the help of a friend, simply transpose the instructions below.

- Lift the collar and drape the bow tie around with adjusters (if any) inside at the back, and the right end hanging a touch lower than the left.

- Cross the long end over the short, under and up through the neck hole.

- Form a loop outwards with the short end so that you have half the 'bow' sticking out to the left, with the remainder of the short end sticking out to the right. Drop the long end down over the front.

- Grasping the long end at the middle, bring it up and push through the middle knot at the back, forming a similar sized bow as you do so on the right-hand side.

- Put a forefinger in each loop and gently adjust. If the bow tie is too loose, pull undone, shorten at the back and tie again.

LOOKING AFTER YOUR TIE
Always hang your tie up, and undo any knots to avoid permanent creasing.

If you are packing a tie, roll it up before putting it in your bag.

Do not dry clean your tie. Dab any stains with a clean napkin dipped in soda water or sprinkle the spot with talcum powder.

AT THE TAILOR

The tailor will ask questions to establish what you want, the climate you'll wear it in, and the function you need it for. They will take your posture and personality into account, so try to be natural, and don't feel uncomfortable about any physical flaws.

The tailor will take a series of measurements with your jacket off – 'direct measure'. Stand in front of the mirror with your shoulders back and legs slightly apart. The tailor will feel inside the waistband for your hip bone – this is generally mid-belt point – and use this as the starting point for measurements.

The pattern will be cut (known as 'striking') according to your particular measurements, and the suit 'basted' (tacked together) for the first or 'base' fitting. At this stage there is no lining, and the suit is very much a work in progress. New measurements will be taken with the suit on; it is then ripped apart and re-basted to a new pattern.

The second fitting is the 'forward stage'. After this the suit will be finished properly and will begin to look more wearable.

For a first suit there will be 3–5 fittings, with perhaps 2–3 weeks between each. Once a tailor has your pattern the process is quicker. With sufficient resources, a suit can be made in six weeks (or less if you can afford to pay enough). It will last more than 20 years.

JACKETS
Single-breasted jackets give a slimmer silhouette and can have one, two or three buttons (with two or three, you don't do up the bottom button). A single button gives cleaner, slimmer lines.

Double-breasted jackets are more formal and give a chunkier shape. These have four or six buttons; do up the lower four, or leave one of the bottom two undone.

TROUSERS
These can be plain or with one or two pleats, which are more roomy and comfortable and better for larger men. Turn-ups go in and out of fashion; see what looks best.

TAILORS' SERVICES
- Made-to-measure: choose whatever you want in any style – a long-term investment.
- Custom service: choose from a ready-to-wear range, but choose the material. The suit will be machine-made, but fitted for basic alterations.
- Ready-to-wear: machine-made, with no alterations.
- Alterations: some tailors make alterations to suits bought elsewhere – these will include putting darts in the jacket to narrow the waist, shortening sleeves, and turning up trousers.

AFTERCARE
Dry cleaning ruins suits – many tailors will hand press suits if you take them back, which will give them a far longer life.

If this isn't possible, steam them: hang them outside to get rid of smoky smells, then hang up in the bathroom for a few days.

If you must dry clean your suit, try not to do it too often.

With shirts, look at the label before washing and soak stains first. Iron upwards on the collar and cuffs, avoiding the tips, which can become shabby if ironed carelessly.

THE PERFECT SHAVE

PROFESSIONAL SHAVES

Book to be sure of an appointment. When you arrive, you will be seated in a reclining seat and asked to take off your tie and undo the top button of your shirt.

You will be given a towel or gown to protect your clothes.

Skin food (often containing rosewater as this has healing properties for sensitive skin) will be applied to the skin. This nourishes and moisturises the skin, as when you shave you take the top, dry layer of skin off too. It will also make the hairs softer, which makes it easier to get a closer shave.

A hot towel is laid over the face and neck and pressed gently against the skin. This opens the pores and pushes the hair follicles so that they are more exposed.

Traditionalists will use a hard shaving soap or soft cream, but never aerosols (anything from a can will have alcohol in it, which closes up the pores). Shaving cream contains glycerine, which softens the hairs. Almond is good for rich moisturising.

Shaving soap is applied with a badger brush; badgers are the only animals whose fur retains water and heat, which is then transferred to the face during the shave. Softer fur from the belly or muzzle is called 'super-badger' by barbers – it is more porous, making for a better shave.

The barber uses an open or straight-edge razor and shaves with the grain as this causes less irritation. The best shave is achieved using a very sharp blade, and pressing lightly.

The barber will shave from the sideburn down one cheek, repeat this on the other side, and then move on to the neck area and chin.

The upper lip is shaved last as it has the thickest hairs, so the longer the cream is left on the softer they'll be.

Any cuts or nicks may be dabbed with a styptic pencil – this contains concentrated alum, stopping the blood flow and closing up pores.

Another hot towel is used to remove any excess soap.

Another layer of skin food or balm is then applied – perhaps with lime this time to wake the customer up. More moisturiser may also be applied.

On really hot days, an ultra-cold towel might be applied for extra refreshment.

YOUR OWN SHAVE

Go with the grain, not against. Remember to moisturise well before and after.

Razor blades should be very sharp – they may last about 1–2 weeks depending on how hirsute you are.

Either change your safety razor frequently, or use a leather and canvas 'strop' to sharpen your open blade razor.

Avoid electric razors – dry shaving means there will be no moisture in the skin, increasing the chance of irritation and a shaving rash.

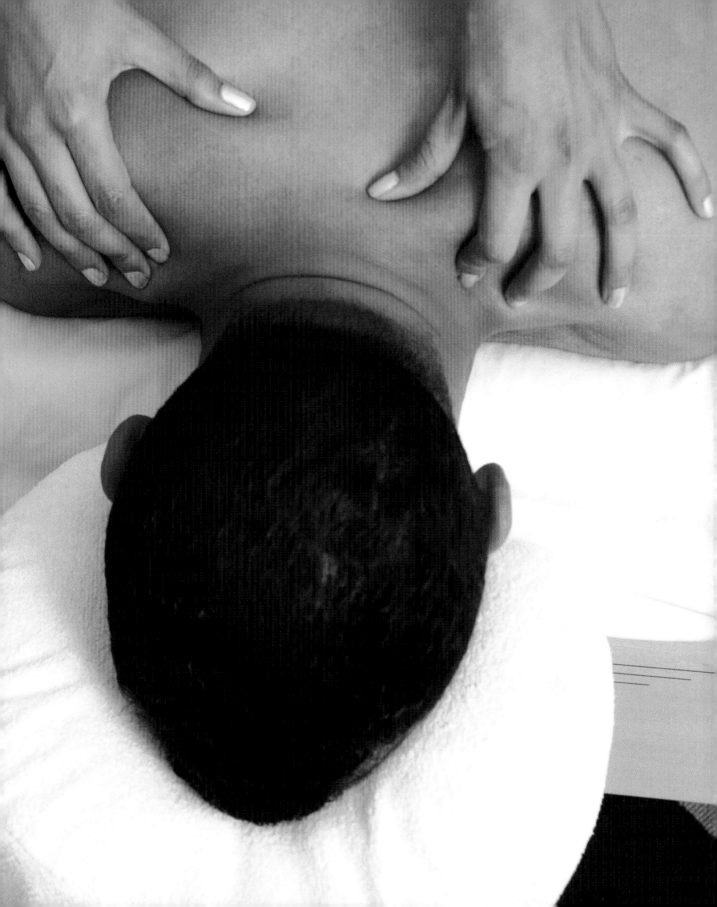

SPA SECRETS

THE BASICS
Make an appointment at least one week ahead, especially for popular weekends and lunchtimes.

Staff tend to be mostly female but you will usually be offered a choice of male or female therapist. Requesting a particular therapist is acceptable as it is good to build up loyalty/trust.

Most spas let customers book by email. Some salons will send a text to remind you about your appointment. Stick to your appointments, or you may be blacklisted for forgetting.

When you arrive, you will have to give details of allergies, injuries and medical conditions.

The best spas offer a (non-alcoholic) drink while you're waiting and newspapers or internet facilities – expect to pay for these extra attentions.

A therapist will generally collect you from the waiting area and take you to a treatment room. Once there, they will explain the treatments, before leaving you to undress.

MASSAGE
All clothes should be taken off except underpants – female masseurs may be uncomfortable with full nudity or it may be stipulated in the house rules. The spa will offer disposable underwear if you are going commando.

Once you are lying down the therapist will return to the treatment room. All areas not being worked on will usually be covered with a towel.

Most therapists will be able to spot problem areas or injuries. Most men put a lot of strain on their back and shoulders, so ask that extra attention be paid to these problem areas if required.

Showers are usually possible afterwards, and make sure you drink plenty of water after the massage.

FACIAL
This is a good way of making the face feel alive – it is great first thing in the morning or after long-haul flight. Make sure you drink water during and after the facial – the beneficial effects of the treatment will be negated if you are dehydrated.

You will be asked to take your shirt off, and a towel will be placed over your chest.

A facial may feature some or all of the following: cleansing, steaming, pore extractions, full-face massage (especially the jawline), a mask, cleanse, moisturise.

You may be offered a foot or hand massage while your face is being cleansed.

There is bound to be advice about products or procedures (i.e. opportunities to sell). Don't be embarrassed about asking, but equally don't feel pressured to buy anything.

OTHER TREATMENTS
Manicures, pedicures and waxing for men are all becoming more common. It is advisable to shower before waxing. You may be able to remain partially clothed if you wish. Ask questions and make sure you understand what the therapist is doing.

GYM ETIQUETTE

THE BASICS
Don't be precious about nudity in the changing rooms.

If you don't want to risk losing things, put them in a locker – the gym will not accept responsibility for stolen items.

Kit should be reasonably clean and decent – avoid revealing shorts and never go bare-chested or barefoot.

Mobiles must be silent or left in lockers; take calls outside. Some gyms ban mobiles.

Make sure you have an adequate supply of water with you, and keep drinking.

Music through headphones should not be audible to others. If you are watching the big TV screens, only change the channel if no one else is watching.

WORKING OUT
Don't check other people's progress or try to race them, and don't stare at girls working out.

Don't offer advice on anyone else's workout. If they wanted advice, they'd get a personal trainer.

MACHINES
Don't 'save' machines at busy times (for yourself or for friends) by leaving your stuff draped on them.

If you need a quick break, pause the machine but stay on it. If you see people waiting, limit your time on that machine to 30 minutes.

If someone is leaving a set of weights you want next, check that they have finished and aren't just having a stretch between repetitions.

If they seem to be resting on their laurels for a prolonged period, wait a few moments before asking if you can swap spaces.

After your workout, wipe any sweaty marks from the machine – most gyms have paper towels available for this.

If you have added weights to your machine, put them back on the communal stack when you have finished.

If you see a woman having difficulty with adjusting her weights, ask if you can help, but don't be pushy.

CLASSES
Signing up for classes means making the effort to be there or calling to cancel – there may be someone else who wants the space.

Be on time for classes and if you arrive late, stay at the back and don't disrupt others.

If you need to leave during the class, choose a quiet moment and make your exit quickly.

PICTURE CREDITS

ACKNOWLEDGEMENTS

Debrett's would like to thank:

The Ritz Club

Morton's Club

Michael Finlay at Geo F. Trumper

Gentlemen's Tonic

Harvey Nichols Personal Shopping

Ranald Macdonald of Boisdale of Belgravia and Floridita

Richard Anderson of Savile Row

The Refinery, Mayfair

Special thanks to Charlie MacDermot-Roe, Michael Bell and Thomas Bryant.

The author would like to thank:

Jo Bryant, for her unflappable editing skills, Eleanor Mathieson, whose first class research left no procedural stone unturned and Elizabeth Wyse, whose patience and good humour made the project such a pleasure.

INDEX

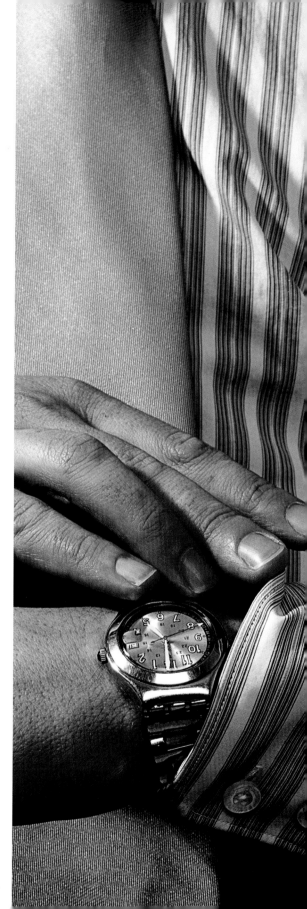